Olympic Games
through a lens

Published by Time Out Guides Ltd, a wholly owned subsidiary of Time Out Group Ltd.
Time Out and the Time Out logo are trademarks of Time Out Group Ltd.

10 9 8 7 6 5 4 3 2

This edition first published in Great Britain in 2011 by Ebury Publishing
A Random House Group Company
20 Vauxhall Bridge Road, London SW1V 2SA

Random House Australia Pty Limited 20 Alfred Street, Milsons Point, Sydney, New South Wales 2061, Australia
Random House New Zealand Limited 18 Poland Road, Glenfield, Auckland 10, New Zealand
Random House South Africa (Pty) Limited Isle of Houghton, Corner Boundary Road & Carse O'Gowrie,
Houghton 2198, South Africa

Random House UK Limited Reg. No. 954009

Distributed in USA by Publishers Group West
1700 Fourth Street, Berkeley, California 94710

Distributed in Canada by Publishers Group Canada
250A Carlton Street, Toronto, Ontario M5A 2L1

For further distribution details, see www.timeout.com

ISBN: 978-1-84670-238-9

A CIP catalogue record for this book is available from the British Library

Printed and bound by Firmengruppe APPL, aprinta druck, Wemding, Germany

The Random House Group Limited supports The Forest Stewardship Council (FSC®), the leading international forest
certification organisation. Our books carrying the FSC label are printed on FSC® certified paper. FSC is the only forest
certification scheme endorsed by the leading environmental organisations, including Greenpeace. Our paper procurement
policy can be found at www.randomhouse.co.uk/environment

Time Out carbon-offsets all its flights with Trees for Cities (www.treesforcities.org).

Time Out Guides Limited
Universal House
251 Tottenham Court Road
London W1T 7AB
Tel + 44 (0)20 7813 3000
Fax + 44 (0)20 7813 6001
Email guides@timeout.com
www.timeout.com

Editorial
Editor Cath Phillips
Proofreader Tamsin Shelton
Indexer William Crow

Managing Director Peter Fiennes
Editorial Director Ruth Jarvis
Business Manager Dan Allen
Editorial Manager Holly Pick

Design
Art Director Scott Moore
Art Editor Pinelope Kourmouzoglou
Senior Designer Kei Ishimaru
Group Commercial Designer Jodi Sher

Picture Desk
Picture Editor Jael Marschner
Acting Deputy Picture Editor Liz Leahy
Picture Desk Assistant/Researcher Ben Rowe

Advertising
New Business & Commercial Director Mark Phillips
Magazine & UK Guides Commercial Director
  St John Betteridge
Account Managers Jessica Baldwin, Michelle Daburn,
  Ben Holt
Production Controller Chris Pastfield
Copy Controller Alison Bourke

Marketing
Sales & Marketing Director, North America
  & Latin America Lisa Levinson
Senior Publishing Brand Manager Luthfa Begum
Guides Marketing Manager Colette Whitehouse
Group Commercial Art Director Anthony Huggins
Marketing Co-ordinator Alana Benton

Production
Group Production Manager Brendan McKeown
Production Controller Katie Mulhern

Time Out Group
Director & Founder Tony Elliott
Chief Executive Officer David King
Chief Operating Officer Aksel Van der Wal
Group Financial Director Paul Rakkar
Group General Manager/Director Nichola Coulthard
Time Out Communications Ltd MD David Pepper
Time Out International Ltd MD Cathy Runciman
Time Out Magazine Ltd Publisher/MD Mark Elliott
Group Commercial Director Graeme Tottle
Group IT Director Simon Chappell
Group Marketing Director Andrew Booth

Contributors Simon Coppock, William Crow, Sarah Thorowgood, Jamie Warburton, Yolanda Zappaterra.

The Editor would like to thank Caroline Theakstone at Getty Images; all at LOCOG.

Photography Getty Images, www.gettyimages.com.
Getty Images is Official Photographic Agency for the 2012 London Games.
Cover and page 3: Olympic Torchbearer John Mark at the London 1948 Olympic Games.

Contents

Introduction

What's the most famous photograph in Olympic history? It depends on who you ask. Some might say Dorando Pietri staggering across the finishing line, helped by officials, at the end of the Marathon at the London 1908 Games. Others might nominate Usain Bolt showboating as he crosses the finish line, metres ahead of the opposition, to win the 100m at the Beijing 2008 Games. And others still the Black Power salute given by Tommie Smith and John Carlos on the podium at Mexico City 1968. All these photos can be found in this book, together with others that typify the spirit of the Olympic Games.

Olympic Games through a lens presents a pictorial survey of all the Summer Olympic Games to date, in chronological order from the Athens 1896 Games to the Beijing 2008 Games. The focus is, inevitably, on individual competitors: the gold medallists, record breakers and outstanding athletes whose achievements have passed into sporting legend. There's Jesse Owens, for example, four-times gold medallist and scourge of Adolf Hitler at the Berlin 1936 Games; Olga Korbut, the diminutive and tearful Soviet gymnast who became an overnight sensation at the Munich 1972 Games; and Michael Phelps, the phenomenal swimmer whose haul of 16 Olympic medals (14 of them gold) makes him the most successful male Olympian of all time. You will have seen many of these stars performing live on television (or possibly even in the flesh), though some predate the advent of TV and are no longer household names: who remembers Archie Hahn, the 'Milwaukee Meteor' and star of St Louis 1904, even though his record for the 200m stood for 28 years?

Most of the athletes pictured are male, although women have taken part in Olympic competition since Paris 1900. Concern over the fragility of the female physique meant that women athletes weren't allowed to run further than 200m until Rome 1960, and the number of events they were allowed to compete in was limited. The introduction of events for women has trailed behind those for men; the first women's Marathon was held at the Los Angeles 1984 Games, though men had been competing at that distance ever since Athens 1896. Women are still in a minority at the Olympic Games – though the gap is narrowing: women made up just over 42 per cent of the competitors at Beijing 2008.

But there's more to Olympic history than individual excellence. So there are pictures of team events too, and less high-profile sports than the perennial favourites of Athletics, Swimming and Gymnastics, including some oddities that didn't last long as official disciplines (Tug-of-war, anyone?). Sporting upsets, such as the still controversial Basketball final between the United States and the Soviet Union at Munich 1972, appear alongside the triumphs.

Some pictures show other elements of the Olympic Games, including iconic stadiums, popular mascots and the dazzling displays of the Opening and Closing Ceremonies. Some reveal that the famous Olympic symbols, now familiar worldwide, haven't been in place for ever: the five interlinked rings were first drawn by Baron Pierre de Coubertin, founder of the modern Olympic movement, in 1913, while the Torch Relay was a progaganda coup for the Berlin 1936 Games. Political boycotts, protests and, in one tragic instance, murder, have also played their role.

One by-product of looking at more than a century of sports photography is to realise how much it has changed. Photography was still in its infancy at the end of the 19th century, so the visual legacy is relatively limited. Most photos were black and white until the mid 1960s, colour thereafter. By the time of the Beijing 2008 Games – in a world of digital media, 24-hours news and worldwide television coverage – the quality, sophistication and sheer number of images is almost overwhelming.

It was also a simpler world in other ways at the time of the early Games. For a start, the technology and equipment were much more basic. Competitors ran in baggy shorts and nailed shoes on gravel tracks or swam in open water in woollen swimming costumes. Vaulting poles were made of wood, and timings were done by hand. The Games themselves were small-scale affairs compared to the lavish spectacles of today. The Paris 1900 Games and St Louis 1904 Games weren't even standalone events, but were shoehorned into already planned exhibitions and, as a result, suffered a loss of identity and prestige. Just 651 athletes representing 12 nations took part at St Louis 1904; a century later, at Athens 2004, there were 10,625 competiors from 201 countries, plus 45,000 volunteers and a media contingent of 21,500.

This is not intended to be a complete or exhaustive history of the Olympic Games. There isn't space for every gold medal winner or iconic event, or to encompass the minutae of Olympic protocol: we just hope that something of the drama, bravery and magnificence of the Olympic Games is evident, and that you enjoy looking at these photographs as much as we enjoyed choosing them.

Cath Phillips, Editor

GETTY IMAGES GALLERY

If you are interested in buying a print of a photograph featured in this book, or of other pictures from Getty Images, contact the Getty Images Gallery, 46 Eastcastle Street, London W1W 8DX, 020 7291 5380, www.gettyimagesgallery.com.

Time Out Guides is proud to be the official book publisher of travel and tourism guides for the **London 2012 Olympic Games and Paralympic Games**.

International Olympic Committee

Members of the International Olympic Committee (IOC) meet in Athens on 10 April 1896 during the inaugural modern Olympic Games; Frenchman Baron Pierre de Coubertin is seated far left, next to the first IOC President, Demetrius Vikelas of Greece. De Coubertin was the driving force behind the revival of the sporting contests of ancient Greece and devoted most of his life to the establishment and continued growth of the modern Olympic movement, serving as IOC President from 1896 until 1925. After his death in 1937, his heart was interred in a marble monument in Olympia, the spiritual and physical homeland of the classical competition.

IOC/Olympic Museum/Allsport/Getty Images

Getty Images

Opening Ceremony

A crowd of 80,000 spectators crammed into the Pan-Athenean Stadium on 6 April 1896 to witness the Opening Ceremony of the first modern Olympic Games in its ancient birthplace, Athens. Greece, Germany, France, Great Britain and the United States were among the 14 nations who took part in the newborn Games, with 241 athletes – men only – competing in 43 events. The white marble stadium had been rebuilt especially (thanks to a donation of nearly a million drachmas by local businessman Georges Averof) on the remains of the stadium that had hosted the ancient Panathenaic Games; it was used again in the 2004 Games for the Archery events and the finish of the Marathon. The anthem composed by Spiros Samaras (music) and Kostis Palamas (lyrics) that was played during the 1896 ceremony became the official Olympic Anthem in 1960.

Spyridon Louis

Spyridon Louis – pictured here in traditional costume holding a Greek flag and standing in front of a painted backdrop of Greece's most recognisable monument, the Acropolis – became a national hero after winning the first Olympic marathon. The race had particular historical significance for the home nation and they were desperate for a Greek to win; when news came that the 23-year-old had taken the lead with four kilometres to go, the 70,000-strong crowd in the stadium erupted with a roar of pride and excitement. He won the race by seven minutes. When the Games were over, Louis returned to his village to work as a shepherd and water carrier, and never raced again. His final Olympic appearance came in 1936, when he carried the national standard for the Greek team at the opening of the Berlin Games.

Popperfoto/Getty Images

100m final

The competitors take their starting positions for the final of the 100m. A standing start was the norm for the time (starting blocks wouldn't be invented for another 30 years), as was the rough surface with ropes separating each lane. American Thomas Burke – pictured second from the left, in a crouched position with his fingertips on the ground – won the race easily in a very respectable 12.0 seconds, ensuring his place in history as the first 100m Olympic champion. He also won the 400m. In fact, the United States did particularly well in the track and field events, winning everything except the 800m, 1500m and the Marathon.

Popperfoto/Getty Images

French cyclists

France dominated the Cycling events in Athens, taking first place in four of the six races. Leon Flameng (left) and Paul Masson (right) pedalled their way to victory in the the purpose-built, open-air Neo Phaliron velodrome, with Flameng winning one gold medal (in the 100km Track event) and Masson three (in the 10,000m Track event, Individual Sprint and 1000m Time Trial). Cycling is one of the rare sports, along with Fencing and Athletics, that has always featured on the Olympic programme.

IOC/Olympic Museum/Allsport/Getty Images

Olympic Golf

Golf has featured only twice in the history of the Olympic Games, at Paris in 1900 and at St Louis four years later – although it's set to make a comeback as an official event in the 2016 Summer Games in Rio de Janeiro. Not all the golfers in Paris realised they were participating in an Olympic competition; the Games were incorporated into the International Universal Exhibition being held in the French capital and lasted five months. There were no Opening and Closing Ceremonies, and little promotion of the Olympic status of the sporting activities. Similar problems occurred in St Louis, and as a result Baron Pierre de Coubertin vowed that subsequent Olympic Games would never again be held in tandem with another event.

Popperfoto/Getty Images

Charlotte Cooper

Women took part in the Olympic Games for the first time in 1900, competing in Croquet, Tennis, Sailing, Golf and Equestrian events. It was a significant but humble start, with only 22 women out of a total of nearly 1,000 athletes. Tennis player Charlotte 'Chattie' Cooper of Great Britain became the first female Olympic champion, thanks to her defeat in the women's singles of French ace Hélène Prévost. Cooper also won the Olympic mixed doubles, partnered by Reggie Doherty. Her Wimbledon championship record was equally impressive; she amassed a total of five women's singles titles between 1895 and 1908, the last at the still record-breaking age of 37.

Popperfoto/Getty Images

Albert Ayat

Fencing was extremely popular in France at the start of the 20th century, and the French dominated the Fencing events at the Paris 1900 Games, winning 15 out of a possible 21 medals. Fencing masters were allowed to participate, even though they were professionals making their living by teaching fencing, as it was the best way to ensure the competition included the world's top swordsmen. Professor Albert Ayat of France won gold in the Amateurs and Masters Epée event, as well as the Masters Epée. The other categories were the Foil and the Sabre, and these three weapons still feature in the 21st-century Olympic programme; Fencing is one of only a handful of sports that has appeared at every Olympic Games to date.

Popperfoto/Getty Images

Alvin Kraenzlein

With a haul of four gold medals, Al Kraenzlein of the United States was the undoubted star of the Paris 1900 Games. He's seen here in action in the 110m hurdles; he also won the 200m Hurdles, the 60m and the Long Jump. Meyer Prinstein, Kraenzlein's team-mate and rival, who was leading the Long Jump after the initial rounds, refused for religious reasons to compete in the final because it was scheduled for a Sunday. When he discovered that Kraenzlein had not only taken part but beaten him – by just 1cm – he was allegedly so enraged that he punched him in the face. As at the Athens 1896 Games, the Americans outshone other nations when it came to Athletics. Particularly notable were Ray Ewry, who came first in all three of the Standing Jump events, and Irving Baxter, who won the High Jump and Pole Vault, and came second behind Ewry in the Standing Jumps.

Popperfoto/Getty Images

Start of the Marathon

As at the previous Games in Paris, the St Louis 1904 Games were not a standalone event. The Games were originally awarded to Chicago, but ended up in St Louis, as part of the World's Fair celebrating the centennial of the United States' purchase of Louisiana from France. Confusion and chaos resulted, with the sporting competitions stretched out over four and a half months. Pictured is the start of the Marathon, eventually won by American runner Thomas Hicks – after some drama. Conditions were difficult: it was an extremely hot day, the course was hilly and dusty, and there was only one source of water en route. Fewer than half the athletes made it to the end. First over the finishing line was Frederick Lorz, also from the US, but it was then discovered that he had hitched a ride in his manager's car for a significant portion of the race. Lorz was disqualified, and the gold medal was awarded to Hicks.

Popperfoto/Getty Images

Introduction of Dumbbells

The St Louis 1904 Games saw the introduction of Boxing, Freestyle Wrestling, Decathlon and Dumbbells events to the Olympic programme and the awarding of gold, silver and bronze medals for first, second and third place. The Dumbbells contest was made up of nine lifting events, followed by a show of strength of the competitor's choice. Silver medallist Frederick Winters of the United States (pictured) opted to perform six one-arm push-ups while carrying 105lb on his back.

Popperfoto/Getty Images

Archibald Hahn

American athlete Archie Hahn, known to fans as the 'Milwaukee Meteor', dominated the sprinting events at St Louis. Not only did he win the 60m, 100m and 200m, but he set an Olympic record of 21.6 seconds in the 200m, a time that would not be bettered for a staggering 28 years. According to the official report of the Games, Hahn was so confident that he teased opponents with 'a tantalising sprint', allowing them to catch up with him before bolting back into the lead and on to victory.

Popperfoto/Getty Images

ST LOUIS 1904

Arrival of King Edward VII

King Edward VII arrives at the Olympic Stadium in White City for the official ceremony to open the London 1908 Games, in which, for the first time, competitors paraded in sportswear behind their country's flag. Originally awarded to Rome, the Games changed location following the eruption of Mount Vesuvius in 1906. Italian funds were diverted to the relief effort and London offered to host the Games instead. Despite the short notice, the 1908 event was extremely well organised and equipped – including the purpose-built stadium – and considered a great success.
Getty Images

London toastmaster

London toastmaster William Knightsmith uses an outsized megaphone to address the masses inside the White City stadium. The Olympic Games were firmly on the international sporting calendar by now, and London 1908 was the best attended Games to date, with 2,008 athletes from 22 nations taking part in 110 different events, and huge crowds watching many of the contests. The British team was by far the largest and, not surprisingly, garnered far more medals than any other country; the United States and Sweden placed second and third.

Getty Images

THE GREAT
MARATHON RACE

Windsor Castle to the Stadium, London,
FRIDAY, JULY 24TH, 1908.

IN view of the fact that this historic Race cannot take place in this Country again for at least thirty years, and bearing in mind that Windsor has been honoured by being selected as the starting place, the Mayor makes an earnest appeal to all Shopkeepers and Employers of Labour in the District to

CLOSE THEIR PREMISES from 1 o'clock to 3.30

on the day, thereby enabling their Employees to witness the Start of what will be a striking and most interesting event in the history of our Town.

About 70 Competitors of all nations will take part in the Race.

Dorando Pietri

The most memorable event at London 1908 was the Marathon, as captured in this world-famous photograph of Italian runner Dorando Pietri being helped over the finishing line by two officials. After entering the Olympic Stadium, Pietri ran the wrong way and collapsed several times before winning the race, but he was disqualified for receiving outside aid and the gold medal was awarded to second-placed American runner John Hayes. But public sympathy was with the valiant Italian, and the following day Queen Alexandra presented him with a special gold cup (pictured left) as a consolation prize. This was also the first time that the length of the modern Marathon – 42km, 195m (26 miles, 385 yards) – was used, to allow the route to start at Windsor Castle and finish in front of the royal box inside the White City stadium. It was accepted as the Olympic Marathon distance at the Paris 1924 Games.

Popperfoto/Getty Images

Getty Images

Tug-of-war

Tug-of-war might seem a strange inclusion on the Olympic programme today, but it featured at all the Games held between 1900 and 1920. Just five teams entered the event in 1908 – Sweden, the United States and three squads of British policemen – which meant that three teams received byes to the semi-finals. In the only quarter-final, the Americans objected to their opponents' footwear: the Liverpool police team (pictured) were wearing their service boots. According to the official report of the Games, the Liverpudlians offered to pull 'in their socks', but the US team withdrew. In the end, the police forces of Great Britain were awarded the gold, silver and bronze medals, with the City of London's law-enforcers defeating Liverpool's bobbies in the final, and the Metropolitan Police finishing third.

Getty Images

Ray Ewry

American Ray Ewry literally leapt to victory in the men's Standing High Jump at London 1908, with a winning jump of 62in. Although athletic success must have seemed an impossibility when he was young – polio confined him to a wheelchair at the age of seven – Ewry became the greatest standing jumper of all time, winning all Olympic events in the discipline from 1900 to 1908. The Standing Triple Jump was withdrawn from Olympic competition after the St Louis 1904 Games, while the Standing High Jump and Standing Long Jump made their final appearances at the 1912 Games in Stockholm. Only four men have ever bettered Ewry's career total of eight Olympic gold medals.

Getty Images

George Larner

Great Britain's George Larner, a Brighton policeman, claimed two gold medals in London, for the 3500m Walk and the 10-mile Walk. He was a rare British winner in the track and field events, which were again dominated by the United States. As well as Ray Ewry, the standout American athletes included Martin Sheridan, who took gold in the two Discus throw events and a bronze in the Standing Long Jump; and Mel Sheppard, a superb middle-distance runner. Sheppard came first in the 800m (with a world record) and the 1500m (with an Olympic record), and was also part of the US team that won the 1600m Medley Relay. It was the first time a relay race had been held at the Olympic Games; handover was by touch, not baton, and it followed the unusual breakdown of 200m, 200m, 400m and 800m.

Getty Images

Wyndham Halswelle

Great Britain's Wyndham Halswelle won the 400m at the London 1908 Games in bizarre circumstances – as the sole participant in the final. The original final was run without lanes, and American athlete John Carpenter blocked Halswelle from overtaking down the final straight. The judges declared the race void, disqualifying Carpenter, and ordered it to be re-run 'in strings'. The two other finalists, also from the United States, refused to take part in protest at Carpenter's dismissal, so Halswelle ran the race on his own.

Getty Images

Henry Taylor

The London 1908 Games saw the Swimming events take place in a purpose-built pool for the first time, instead of in open water. The White City stadium contained a swimming pool inside the running track, with a special folding tower at its edge for the Diving events. The Aquatics events were contested particularly fiercely, and Henry Taylor of Great Britain won three gold medals in the men's Freestyle 400m, 1500m and 4 x 200m Relay. No British athlete would win as many gold medals in one edition of the Games until cyclist Chris Hoy equalled Taylor a century later, at the Beijing 2008 Games.

Popperfoto/Getty Images

Women's Archery

Women were still in a definite minority at the 1908 Games, with only 37 women participants compared to 1,971 men. The women's Archery contest was won by Sybil 'Queenie' Newall of Great Britain, who still has the distinction of being the oldest woman to claim an Olympic gold – at the age of 53 years and 277 days. Women also competed in Tennis, Sailing and Figure Skating (the first time skating featured) and there were gymnastic displays by various female teams from Scandinavia, but these were only an exhibition event and the sport did not achieve full-blown Olympic status until the Amsterdam 1928 Games.

Getty Images

Scandinavian gymnasts

The Norwegian women's Gymnastics team, as well as the men's teams from Norway (top right) and Sweden (bottom right), display their skills at the Stockholm 1912 Games – although the women would have to wait until 1928 to compete officially. The men contested one individual and three team events, the latter following the three methods of Artistic Gymnastics then in use: European, Swedish (won by the Swedes, not surprisingly) and the free system. The Stockholm Games were labelled a 'model of efficiency', and featured such innovations as the use of automatic timing for track events and public address systems. With Japan making its inaugural appearance, it was also the first Games to include delegations from all five continents.

Popperfoto/Getty Images

Jim Thorpe

Described by King Gustav V of Sweden as 'the greatest athlete in the world', Native American Jim Thorpe won both the Pentathlon and Decathlon – new events in Stockholm – by huge margins. He also entered the individual High Jump and Long Jump, and was an accomplished baseball and American football player. It was later discovered that prior to the Games he had received a modest amount of money for playing minor league baseball in North Carolina, an offence against the Olympic rules of amateurship. As a result, Thorpe was stripped of his medals, but in 1982 after years of campaigning, the IOC recognised his achievements and duplicates of his medals were returned to his children.

Getty Images

British women swimmers

Aquatics for women became part of the Olympic Games for the first time in 1912, although there were just three events available: the 100m Freestyle, the 4 x 100m Freestyle Relay and Plain High Diving. The competitions, along with Water Polo and Rowing, took place in Djurgårdsbrunnsviken, a bay near Stockholm city centre. The Great British team (Jennie Fletcher, Bella Moore, Annie Spiers and Irene Steer) secured an easy victory in the relay race over Germany, Austria and Sweden. As only four teams entered, there were no heats, just one race deemed to be the final.

Popperfoto/Getty Images

Hannes Kolehmainen

Hannes Kolehmainen – here leading the final of the men's 10,000m – was the first of a generation of talented middle- and long-distance runners from Finland known as 'the Flying Finns'. At Stockholm 1912 he won gold in the 5000m, 10,000m and Individual Cross-Country events, and ran a world record time in the 3000m Team Race event (though Finland failed to qualify for the final). In the 5000m final, Kolehmainen and his French rival, Jean Bouin, ran a lightning pace shoulder to shoulder, before the Finn edged over the line in 14 minutes, 36.6 seconds – the first formal world record for the distance and just one-tenth of a second ahead of Bouin. The Games official report describes it as the 'most interesting, the severest and the finest long-distance race that has probably ever been witnessed'.

Popperfoto/Getty Images

Oscar Swahn

Swedish marksman Oscar Swahn bagged six medals in three Olympic Games: two golds and a bronze at London 1908, a gold and a bronze at Stockholm 1912 and a silver at Antwerp 1920. At the time of winning his last medal (in the Running Deer, Double Shot Team event), he was an impressive 72 years and 279 days old, which makes him the oldest Olympic medallist to date – as well as the oldest Olympian. Most of the Shooting events that featured at Stockholm 1912, such as the running deer, clay pigeon and military rifle contests, are still on the Olympic programme – though duelling pistols no longer play a part.

IOC/Allsport/Getty Images

Equestrian events

Events featuring riders and horses competing together first featured at the Paris 1900 Games, but it wasn't until the Stockholm 1912 Games that it appeared in a form similar to modern equestrianism. To increase participation, the organisers secured prestigious 'challenge prizes' from European monarchs and noblemen to be awarded to the winner of each of the five events. Sweden dominated on home ground, winning all five except the Individual Jumping prize, which went to Frenchman Jean Cariou. Note the military regalia of the Russian team pictured here: only officers (and therefore only men) were allowed to compete. This restriction was lifted in 1951, and women riders first appeared in 1952.
Popperfoto/Getty Images

Greco-Roman Wrestling

Wrestling is probably the world's oldest competitive sport and was a key fixture of the ancient Olympic Games, so when the modern Games were reborn in 1896, Greco-Roman Wrestling was given a central role as the epitome of classical competition. In the Greco-Roman discipline, wrestlers are allowed to attack only with their upper bodies and arms, and above the waistline of their opponent. Pictured is the middleweight semi-final match in Stockholm between Russia's Martin Klein and Finland's Alfred Asikainen, which lasted a record 11 hours. Klein won, but was too tired from the lengthy battle to continue, so the final was uncontested and Swede Claes Johansson claimed the gold medal.

Popperfoto/Getty Images

STOCKHOLM 1912

Erik Adlerz

Erik Adlerz of Sweden won a silver medal
(in the men's Platform Diving event), helping
his country come second in the overall medals
table at the Antwerp 1920 Games, behind the
United States. The 1916 Games had been
cancelled because of World War I, and Belgium
was awarded the Games in 1920 to make
up for the country's suffering during the war.
Germany, Austria, Hungary, Bulgaria and
Turkey weren't invited, but 29 nations took
part, including New Zealand, which appeared
for the first time under its own flag rather than
as part of a combined team with Australia.
The Opening Ceremony saw some other firsts
too: the swearing of the competitors' Olympic
oath, the release of a flock of doves as a
symbol of peace, and the use of the Olympic
flag with its five rings to signify the union of
the five continents.

Popperfoto/Getty Images

Albert Hill

Great Britain didn't do badly in the track events at the Antwerp 1920 Games. Albert Hill triumphed in the 800m and 1500m (at the age of 31), Percy Hodge won gold in the 3000m Steeplechase and the British team came first in the men's 4 x 400m Relay; the team also garnered a handful of silver and bronze medals. But Antwerp was more significant, in terms of Olympic Athletics history, for marking the debut of Finland's Paavo Nurmi, one of the greatest Olympians of all time. Nurmi took home three golds, but this was just the start of an astounding career that saw him amass a total of 12 Olympic medals between 1920 and 1928 – a record that no other Athletics competitor has overtaken.

Popperfoto/Getty Images

Duke Kahanamoku

Hawaiian-born Duke Kahanamoku won his first Olympic gold medal at the Stockholm 1912 Games, in the 100m Freestyle, a feat he would repeat in 1920 in Antwerp (he's in lane five in the photograph), where he also helped the US to a convincing victory in the 4 x 200m Freestyle Relay. He attempted a hat-trick of 100m Freestyle golds at the Paris 1924 Games, but could only manage second place, thanks to the arrival of another legendary Olympic swimmer, Johnny Weissmuller. Duke's younger brother, Sam, came third. Kahanamoku also travelled the world giving swimming demonstations, during which he would show off his impressive surfing skills – at the time, a sport little known outside Hawaii. He's credited with raising surfing's profile across the world, especially in Australia and southern California, where he appeared in assorted Hollywood movies.

Getty Images

Nedo Nadi

Hailed as one of the greatest fencers of the 20th century, Italian Nedo Nadi (pictured in 1912) won his first Olympic gold at the age of 18 at the Stockholm 1912 Games. Nadi had fencing in his blood; his father was a renowned fencing master and his younger brother, Aldo, also competed in Fencing at Olympic level. At the Antwerp 1920 Games, Nadi's skill and versatility were astonishing: he won all five contests that he entered, taking gold in two individual events (Sabre, Foil) and three Team events (Sabre, Foil, Epée). Nadi's victories at such a young age, in a sport that can take a lifetime to master, earned him the lasting admiration of his fellow competitors, as well as the public. His haul of five gold medals at a single Games remained a record until 1972, when American swimmer Mark Spitz took seven at the Munich Games.

IOC/Allsport/Getty Images

Suzanne Lenglen

Dominating the women's tennis circuit for much of the early 20th century, Suzanne Lenglen of France was as big a personality on the court as she was off it. Nicknamed 'La Divine' by the French press, she was one of sport's first international female stars, winning an astounding number of titles during her career, including six Wimbledon singles championships between 1919 and 1925. She revitalised the women's game with her athletic style of play and adoption of lightweight dresses with exposed forearms and calves. This photograph shows Lenglen playing at the Antwerp 1920 Games, where she took gold in both the women's Singles and the mixed Doubles, and a bronze in the women's Doubles.

Getty Images

ABRAHAMS   SCHOLZ   PADDOCK

JEUX OLYMPIQUES DE 1924

Harold Abrahams

Determined to do well at the Paris 1924 Games, British sprinter Harold Abrahams enlisted the services of coach Sam Mussabini and trained industriously throughout the winter of 1923 and 1924. The relationship between Abrahams and Mussabini is central to *Chariots of Fire*, Hugh Hudson's very popular 1981 film about the Paris 1924 Olympic Games. Abrahams took silver with the British 4 x 100m Relay team and triumphed in the final of the 100m – pictured – in 10.6 seconds, defeating the American favourites Jackson Scholz (who came second) and Charlie Paddock. He also made the 200m final, coming sixth. Abrahams didn't get the chance to defend his Olympic title; his career as a competitive athlete ended prematurely after he broke his leg while long jumping in 1925.
Popperfoto/Getty Images

Eric Liddell

Eric Liddell didn't enter the 100m, his strongest event, at Paris 1924 due to his belief that competing in the heats – scheduled for a Sunday – would be blasphemous. Instead, the 'Flying Scotsman' entered the 200m and 400m and, despite doubts about his ability in these events, took bronze in the 200m and gold in the 400m, the latter with a world record time of 47.6 seconds. Liddell's dilemma, and achievements, were also immortalised in the movie *Chariots of Fire*, which proved a success in its own right by winning four Academy Awards. Liddell later became a missionary in China (like his parents), and died in a Japanese internment camp in 1945.

Popperfoto/Getty Images

Johnny Weissmuller

Swimming's first superstar, Johnny Weissmuller made his Olympic debut at Paris 1924 in some style, winning three golds (in the 100m Freestyle, 400m Freestyle and 4 x 200m Freestyle Relay) and a bronze in the Water Polo competition. Four years later, at the Amsterdam 1928 Games, he retained his Olympic titles in the 100m Freestyle and 4 x 200m Freestyle Relay. The American set 28 world records during his career, with his 1927 record for the 100yd freestyle remaining unbeaten for 17 years. Weissmuller's superiority can be attributed to his novel high-riding technique, flutter kick and head-turning breathing. After swimming, he found further fame as an actor, playing Tarzan of the Apes in 12 movies, and is now the actor most readily associated with the character and his yodelling call.

Popperfoto/Getty Images

Paavo Nurmi

A national hero in Finland and one of only four competitors to have won nine Olympic gold medals (and three silvers), Paavo Nurmi was one of the greatest middle- and long-distance runners of all time. He competed in three Olympic Games (1920, 1924 and 1928) – and would have appeared at Los Angeles 1932, but was banned as a professional by the International Association of Athletics Federations (IAAF) for appearing as the star attraction in athletics meets worldwide. His greatest achievements came at Paris 1924, where he won a staggering five gold medals over the course of four days; the 1500m (pictured), 5000m, 3000m Team Race and both the Individual and Team Cross-Country events. The tally is even more astonishing considering that the finals of the 1500m and 5000m were run less than 45 minutes apart. He also intended to defend the 10,000m title he had won at the Antwerp 1920 Games, but officials refused to enter him on health grounds. Nurmi returned to Finland and responded by setting a 10,000m world record that remained unbeaten for nearly 13 years – and he again claimed the 10,000m gold at the Amsterdam 1928 Games. His final Olympic appearance came in 1952, when he lit the Olympic flame at the Helsinki Games.
IOC/Allsport/Getty Images

Ville Ritola

The successes of Finnish runner Ville Ritola were somewhat overshadowed by those of his fellow countryman and great rival Paavo Nurmi. Ritola came second behind Nurmi in the Individual Cross-Country and 5000m events at Paris 1924, but still took four gold medals (in the 10,000m, the 3000m Steeplechase, the 3000m Team Race and the Cross-Country Team events). The pair met again in the 10,000m final at the Amsterdam 1928 Games, where Nurmi triumphed once more. However, Ritola was victorious in his last Olympic appearance, the final of the 5000m, when he pulled away from his rival on the final bend and won by 15 metres, bringing his career Olympic total to five gold and three silver medals.

Popperfoto/Getty Images

Andrew Charlton

Andrew 'Boy' Charlton of Australia took the gold medal for the 1500m Freestyle in the Paris 1924 Games at the age of just 16, wiping a minute off the world record in the process, as well as a silver (in the 4 x 200m Freestyle Relay) and a bronze (in the 400m Freestyle). Having already made a name for himself in Sydney earlier in 1924 by beating Swedish star Arne Borg, Charlton's remarkable achievement at such a young age secured his place in Australian sporting history. This was an era of legendary male swimmers, with Americans Johnny Weissmuller and Duke Kahanamoku, as well as Borg, all winning medals at Paris 1924. Charlton competed again in the Amsterdam 1928 Games, winning two silver medals but this time missing out on the 1500m gold to his old rival Borg.

Popperfoto/Getty Images

Prince of Wales and Baron de Coubertin

In 1924, Paris hosted the Olympic Games for the second time. The occasion marked the advent of the Games as a global phenomenon: the number of participating nations rose from 29 to 44, coverage of the event was broadcast on radio for the first time, and 625,000 spectators and more than 1,000 journalists attended. Paris 1924 also saw the introduction of the Closing Ceremony as we now know it, with the raising of three flags (for the IOC, the host nation and the host nation of the next Games). Notable visitors included the Prince of Wales (later Edward VIII, fourth from the right) and Baron Pierre de Coubertin (far right), founder of the modern Olympic movement. This would be Baron de Coubertin's last Olympic Games as President of the IOC.

Getty Images

United States team ship

The dilemma of where to house the visiting athletes at the Amsterdam 1928 Games was solved by using the ships in which many teams had arrived. This steam freighter, berthed in Amsterdam harbour, had carried the United States team across the Atlantic, along with 1,000 cases of Coca-Cola (the brand was the Games' first official sponsor). Amsterdam 1928 were notable for a number of innovations in the Opening Ceremony: this was the first occasion on which the Olympic flame was lit (in a cauldron at the top of a specially built tower), and the Parade of Nations was led by the Greek team, with the Dutch coming last. Greece-first, hosts-last has been Olympic protocol ever since.

Gamma-Keystone via Getty Images

Henry Pearce

Rowing champion Henry Robert 'Bobby' Pearce receives his victory laurels for the men's Single Sculls at Amsterdam 1928. Facing tight competition from Kenneth Myers of the United States and David Colet of Great Britain in the quarter-final, Pearce nevertheless had the sang-froid to pause momentarily to allow a family of ducks to cross his lane before he went on to win the heat and, ultimately, the gold medal. The son and grandson of former Australian sculling champions, Pearce successfully defended his title at the Los Angeles 1932 Games.

Popperfoto/Getty Images

AMSTERDAM 1928

Lord Burghley

At the Amsterdam 1928 Games, David George Brownlow Cecil, Lord Burghley, became the first non-American to win gold in the 400m Hurdles, his time of 53.4 seconds equalling the world record. The Briton went on to win silver in the 4 x 400m Relay at the next Games in Los Angeles – although whether his mother repeated her act of kindness for the latter race of providing silk shorts to prevent chafing is not recorded. Later, the 'Leaping Lord' became a Conservative MP and a member of the IOC. He was a key organiser of the London 1948 Games.

Popperfoto/Getty Images

Olympic Football

Until the inaugural World Cup in 1930, football's only intercontinental tournament was the Olympic Games. Uruguay were the first South American team to play Olympic Football, at the Paris 1924 Games – when they won. Four years later, they were joined by Argentina, Mexico and Chile (pictured is Chile's goalkeeper, in the cap, failing to keep Portugal from scoring). In the 1928 final, Uruguay drew 1-1 with Argentina, but won the replay 2-1 to retain their gold medal. The Uruguayans were a revelation, introducing a game based on free-flowing movement and inventive passes rather than brute physicality. Their talismanic player was midfielder José Andrade, the first internationally acclaimed black footballer. Andrade also starred in the first World Cup (hosted and won by Uruguay), despite the permanent eye damage he had sustained in a collision with a goalpost during the Amsterdam 1928 Games.

Getty Images

Canadian women athletes

Amsterdam 1928 was a landmark Olympic Games for women. The number of female participants was double the previous Games (although the total was only 277, in comparison to 2,606 men), and for the first time they were allowed to compete in Team Gymnastics and a limited number of track and field events. The Canadian Athletics team was the strongest; sprinters Myrtle Cook, Jane Bell, Fanny Rosenfeld and Ethel Smith, middle-distance runner Jean Thompson, and high jumper Ethel Catherwood were so highly thought of they were nicknamed the 'Matchless Six'. Cook (far left) was disqualified from the 100m final after two false starts, but Rosenfeld and Smith took silver and bronze behind Elizabeth Robinson of the United States. The Canadian women also won two gold medals: in the 4 x 100m Relay (in a world record time of 48.4 seconds) and the high jump. None of the six competed in another Olympic Games.

Popperfoto/Getty Images

Ethel Catherwood

Canadian high jumper Ethel Catherwood (nicknamed the 'Saskatoon Lily') got as much press attention for her looks as for her athleticism at the Amsterdam 1928 Games, but she was a fierce competitor. She would psych out opponents by competing in her tracksuit until she failed a jump, then strip down to shorts to clear the bigger jumps. The strategy won her gold. Catherwood was also a talented baseball player and a fine javelin thrower; she won the Javelin gold at the 1930 British Empire Games, held in Ontario.

Getty Images

Opening Ceremony

As a result of the Great Depression and poor transport links to California, athletes' attendance at the Los Angeles 1932 Games was less than half that of the previous Games in Amsterdam. However, the scale of the event was extraordinary, as shown in this photo of the Olympic Stadium (now the Los Angeles Memorial Coliseum), where 100,000 spectators enjoyed the Opening Ceremony. The efficiency of the competition also impressed. Between 1900 and 1928 no Olympic Games had lasted fewer than 79 days – Los Angeles reduced this to just 16, setting a precedent for future Games, which have since varied in duration from 15 to 18 days. Other innovations occurred at the medal presentation ceremonies: the winners mounted a podium and their countries' flags were raised.

Popperfoto/Getty Images

Olympic Village

The first modern Olympic Village was constructed for the Los Angeles 1932 Games in the suburb of Baldwin Hills, with the intention of uniting athletes from different nations in a 'true expression of the Olympic doctrine and ideals'. In previous Games, each National Olympic Committee (NOC) had been responsible for organising accommodation. The Village, a temporary affair that was torn down after the Games, provided housing in bungalows, as well as post and telegraph offices, a bank, a hospital, an entertainment centre and several canteens. It was for male athletes only; the 126 women participants stayed at the luxury Chapman Park Hotel on Wilshire Boulevard in downtown LA.

Popperfoto/Getty Images

LOS ANGELES 1932

Georges Miez

Swiss artistic gymnast Georges Miez first competed in the Olympic Games in 1924, winning a bronze in the Team All-Around event at the age of 19. He returned to the Summer Games three more times – a remarkable feat in itself – winning medals on each occasion: three golds (including the Individual All-Around event) and a silver at Amsterdam 1928, another silver at Los Angeles 1932, and a gold and a silver at Berlin 1936.
Popperfoto/Getty Images

Eddie Tolan

The first African-American to claim the label of the world's fastest human, Eddie Tolan on both the 100m and the 200m at the Los Angeles 1932 Games. Here, he's winning the 200m in front of his team-mates George Simpson (pictured) and Ralph Metcalfe; Metcalfe got silver in the 100m too. The 1930s was the beginning of an Olympic golden era for the United States, especially in track and field events. Los Angeles 1932 alone saw them take gold in 16 of the 29 Athletics events; it would have been a clean sweep for the American women, but for Polish star Stanisława Wałasiewicz, who won the 100m. In total, the US won 103 medals; the next best country was Italy with a mere 36.

Gamma-Keystone via Getty Images

Aquatics events

Divers practise at the 10,000-seater art deco Olympic Swimming stadium in Los Angeles. The United States comprehensively trounced all competition in the Diving, winning every single medal in both the men's and women's springboard and platform events – it was a domination of the sport that was only cracked in the 1980s by the Chinese. The American women's Swimming team also fared well, taking gold in four out of five disciplines, but it was Japan who cleaned up in the men's events. Feeling the absence of swimming hero Johnny Weissmuller, the US only won gold in the 400m Freestyle event, thanks to Buster Crabbe. (Coincidentally, Crabbe, like Weissmuller, went on to star in many Hollywood films, most famously as Flash Gordon in the 1936 science fiction film serial.)
Popperfoto/Getty Images

Mildred Didrikson

Multi-talented Mildred 'Babe' Didrikson captured the heart of the host nation at the Los Angeles 1932 Games, winning gold in the Javelin (with her first throw, which was also an Olympic record) and the 80m Hurdles (with a new world record) and silver in the High Jump. If women had been allowed to enter more than three events, she would probably have claimed more medals. It was the American's only Olympic Games; soon after, she turned her attention to golf. Known under her married name Zacharias, she became the most famous and successful female golfer of her day, winning numerous tournaments and awards during a 20-year career.

Getty Images

Torch Relay

Although an Olympic flame had first featured at the Amsterdam 1928 Games, the Berlin 1936 Games inaugurated the tradition of the Torch Relay. The idea came from organiser Dr Carl Diem, who arranged for a flaming torch to be carried 3,187km from Olympia (the historic site of the ancient Olympic Games) to Berlin's Olympiastadion, where runner Fritz Schilgen – the last of 3,331 Torchbearers – lit the cauldron. Nowadays, the Olympic flame is lit using only the rays of the sun, focused by a special parabolic mirror. It remains alight for the duration of each Games, and is extinguished at the Closing Ceremony.

Getty Images

Hitler arrives at the Games

The Berlin 1936 Games will always be remembered for Adolf Hitler's attempt – and failure – to turn Olympic competition into propaganda for his racial theories about Aryan superiority. The Germans' stage management of the occasion, from the breathtaking stadia to the 25 television rooms that were opened to the Berlin public for viewing the events, was detailed and elaborate. Upwards of four million tickets were sold to spectators. Germany dominated the cultural events (architecture, art and literature competitions were run), just as they did the sport, but the headlines focused on the outstanding achievements of one particular black athlete.

Gamma-Keystone via Getty Images

Jesse Owens

Although the individual medals table was topped by German gymnasts Konrad Frey (who won six) and Alfred Schwarzmann (who won five), the popular hero of Berlin 1936 – and a sporting legend ever since – was the African-American athlete Jesse Owens. Holder of six world records since 1935, Alabama-born Owens was still at the peak of his powers. He not only won gold in the 100m (left), 200m, 4 x 100m Relay and the Long Jump (right), but set three new world records in the process, including a time in the 4 x 100m Relay that remained the world's best for two decades. Recognised as a hero on the streets of Berlin (much, it is said, to the Führer's irritation), he returned to a United States that was still segregated along racial lines.

Popperfoto/Getty Images

Getty Images

Luz Long and Jesse Owens

German athlete Luz Long converses with Jesse Owens, to whom he came second in the Long Jump. Owens fouled in two of his three qualifying jumps; had he missed his last attempt, the American would have been out of the competition. Years after the event, Owens recalled that Long had recommended he should jump from further behind the take-off board – correctly judging that the qualifying distance was within Owens' grasp, even with this slight handicap. For this display of sportsmanship, Long was awarded the Pierre de Coubertin medal. The two athletes never again met after the Games (Long died in a military hospital during World War II), but they remained in cordial contact: indeed, Owens was invited to be best man at the marriage of Long's son.

Popperfoto/Getty Images

Harold Whitlock

Great Britain won four events at Berlin 1936, including the 50km Walk, thanks to Harold Whitlock (seen here entering the stadium at the end of the race). Tall and with a dashing fighter-ace moustache, he was among the favourites and won easily, despite suffering severe illness en route. The Hendon-born mechanic returned to compete at Helsinki 1952 at the age of 48, where he finished in an impressive 11th place – the oldest British man to have competed in an Olympic Games.

Popperfoto/Getty Images

Marjorie Gestring

The 1936 Games were kind to American divers: they took ten of the dozen medals on offer, missing out on just two bronzes. But the real sensation was Marjorie Gestring, a 13-year-old springboard diver from Los Angeles, who beat her team-mates (including defending champion Dorothy Poynton-Hill) to the gold from the 3m board. Gestring remains the youngest woman to have won gold at a Summer Games, while another competitor at Berlin – 12-year-old swimmer Inge Sørensen from Denmark, who took bronze in the 200m Breaststroke – is the youngest medallist in an individual Olympic event.

Gamma-Keystone via Getty Images

Olympic rings

Young women take part in a display at the Berlin 1936 Games. The five interlaced Olympic rings – blue, yellow, black, green, red – were first seen at the top of a 1913 letter by Baron Pierre de Coubertin, drawn and coloured by hand. By June 1914, he had incorporated them into a flag with a white background, with all six colours taken to represent every nation, since one or more of those colours appeared at that time on every national flag. It was never de Coubertin's intention that each of the five rings should invidually represent a continent. This symbol of international unity is now recognised across the world.

Popperfoto/Getty Images

Cornelius Johnson

Jesse Owens rightly claimed the headlines at Berlin 1936 with his four golds, but the African-American contingent of the United States team was extremely strong across the track and field events. The team captured all the men's High Jump medals, with both the winner Cornelius Johnson and silver medallist David Albritton being black. So too were Ralph Metcalfe and Matthew 'Mack' Robinson, who took silver behind Owens in the 100m and 200m sprints, respectively; Metcalfe also won gold as part of Owens' 4 x 100m Relay team. Not a bad return for athletes who had been dismissed before the Games by one Nazi newspaper as mere 'auxiliaries' to their white team-mates.

Popperfoto/Getty Images

Leni Riefenstahl

The first Games to be broadcast on live (closed-circuit) television, Berlin 1936 was also popularised by one of the most remarkable sports films ever made. *Olympia* was a formal and aesthetic triumph, with director Leni Riefenstahl (pictured here with cameraman Walter Frentz) using outlandish angles and new techniques to find extraordinary beauty in the Games. Her film is no documentary account of sporting events, however, and has been attacked for glorifying the Nazi regime.
Getty Images

Opening Ceremony

On 29 July 1948, just three years after the end of World War II and 12 years since the previous Olympic Games, King George VI opened the London Games at Wembley Stadium in front of 85,000 spectators. The city had been selected as host just two years earlier and was still ravaged by the effects of the war. Despite such difficulties, the Games were a huge success, and the Opening Ceremony a very English affair complete with parading Guardsmen, army bands and boy scouts, the release of 2,500 pigeons and a 21-gun salute by the Royal Horse Artillery. Just over 4,000 athletes took part; Germany, Japan and the USSR were not invited, but many countries were represented for the first time, including Burma, Ceylon, Lebanon, Syria and Venezuela.

Popperfoto/Getty Images

Bob Mathias

American high-school student Bob Mathias was just 17 when his track coach suggested he take up the Decathlon. Less than four months later, Mathias qualified for the United States team for the London 1948 Games. He won the Decathlon, despite fouling in the shot put because of his unfamiliarity with the rules and having to finish the competition in pouring rain and semi-darkness in a deserted stadium. He's still the youngest male winner of an Olympic Athletics gold. At the Helsinki 1952 Games, Mathias broke his own world record to became the first repeat winner of the Decathlon – a distinction he shares with just one other athlete, Great Britain's Daley Thompson.

Popperfoto/Getty Images

Micheline Ostermeyer

Multi-talented French athlete Micheline Ostermeyer picked up a discus for the first time just a few weeks before winning the gold medal in London. She also took the gold in the Shot Put – 1948 was the first time the event was open to women. With a bronze in the High Jump too, she proved herself to be an impressively versatile, and natural, athlete, but her true passions lay in music. She had studied piano at the Conservatoire de Paris before the London Games, and went on to have a concert career; after her Olympic victories, she gave an impromptu Beethoven recital in the women's housing centre. 'Sport taught me to relax,' she said, 'and the piano gave me strong biceps.'

Gamma-Keystone via Getty Images

LONDON 1948

Fanny Blankers-Koen

At the London 1948 Games, Dutchwoman Fanny Blankers-Koen – aged 30 and a mother of two – was written off as being past it. She had been robbed of the chance of competing in two Olympic Games at her peak (both the 1940 and 1944 Games were cancelled because of World War II), but nevertheless trounced the opposition by winning all four Athletics events for which she entered: the 100m (bottom right), 200m (left), 80m Hurdles (top right) and 4 x 100m Relay. She could have won more medals – she held the world records in both the Long Jump and High Jump – but for the rule limiting women to three individual events. On her triumphant return to Amsterdam, the 'Flying Housewife' was presented with a bicycle in order that she might 'go through life at a slower pace'.

Getty Images
Popperfoto/Getty Images

100m final

The first Olympic photo-finish revealed a shock: Harrison 'Bones' Dillard of the United States (at the bottom) crossed the line first in 10.3 seconds, followed a tenth of a second later by fellow American Henry 'Barney' Ewell, the favourite for the race. Both men took gold when the US won the 4 x 100m Relay. Dillard was more renowned as a hurdler, but had failed to qualify at the trials for the 1948 Games; he made amends in the 1952 Games in Helsinki, where he was victorious in the 110m Hurdles and again in the Relay. Dillard's sporting ambition had been fired by a victory parade in his native Cleveland for Jesse Owens after the Berlin 1936 Games; Owens himself encouraged Dillard to take up hurdling and later gave him the spikes he had worn in Berlin.

Popperfoto/Getty Images

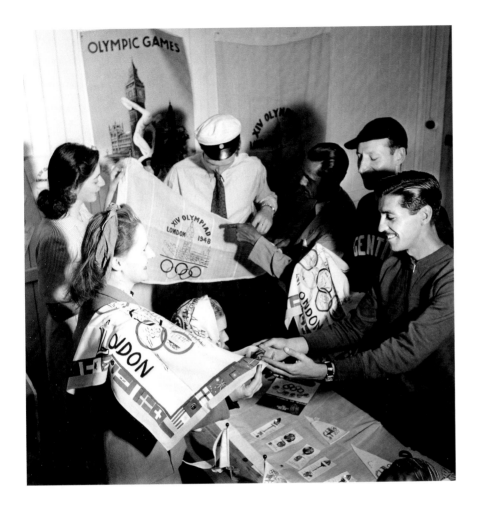

Olympic souvenirs

Scarves, posters, tea towels and other souvenirs on sale at the Olympic training camp in Uxbridge, Middlesex. Housing was in very short supply in post-war Britain, so the participating athletes were put up in schools, colleges and RAF camps (Uxbridge took 1,500, including the US team); bedding was supplied, but not towels. Rationing was still in place, so many teams arrived with food parcels, and the British athletes had to make their own kit. But the 'Austerity Games', as they became known, were also characterised by great cameraderie, a defiant 'can do' attitude and a determination to succeed, in the sports arena and beyond, that typified the Olympic spirit.

Popperfoto/Getty Images

Gaston Reiff

London's weather proved predictably unpredictable during the 1948 Games. The competition began on 29 July with temperatures soaring into the mid 30s°C (it was the hottest day on record since 1911), but the weather then turned wet and windy, disrupting schedules and affecting attendance levels for much of the rest of the Games. Gaston Reiff managed to win the 5000m despite the wet conditions and an astonishing late burst from the great Czech runner Emil Zátopek (who had won the 10,000m three days earlier); Zátopek came storming down the last straight to the roars of the crowd, but Reiff finished first by 0.2 seconds. He was the first Belgian to win gold in an Olympic Athletics event.

Getty Images

Károly Takács

Before World War II, Hungarian Károly Takács was a world-class pistol shooter. In September 1938, a faulty grenade caused him to lose his right hand – his pistol hand. Undaunted, he taught himself to shoot with his left. Ten years later, he competed at London 1948, where he surprised everybody by winning the 25m Rapid Fire Pistol event, beating the favourite, Carlos Díaz Sáenz Valiente of Argentina, and also setting a new world record. He repeated his success in the same event at the Helsinki 1952 Games.

Allsport/Getty Images

Olympic Tower

This monolithic tower stands 72m tall at the south end of the Olympic Stadium in Helsinki. The city had been due to host the Games in 1940 and the stadium was ready for use as early as summer 1938, but the outbreak of World War II meant that both the 1940 and 1944 events were cancelled. When a host was sought for the Olympic Games in 1952, Helsinki was the obvious choice. With a capacity of 70,000, the stadium was the venue for the Opening and Closing Ceremonies, as well as the Athletics competitions, the Equestrian events and Football. Today, it's home to Finland's national football team and the tower is open to visitors, offering spectacular views across Helsinki.

Getty Images

Patricia McCormick

American Pat McCormick turns gracefully on her way to winning Olympic gold in both the Platform and Springboard events at the Helsinki 1952 Games; the United States took all four golds across the men's and women's events. McCormick repeated her clean sweep four years later at the Melbourne/Stockholm 1956 Games, making her the only woman ever to win the Diving double. McCormick's daughter, Kelly, also became a medal-winning Olympic diver in the 1980s. Diving was introduced to the Olympic programme at the St Louis 1904 Games, with women allowed to compete from Stockholm 1912, and Synchronised Diving first appearing at Sydney 2000.

Getty Images

Debut of the USSR

Helsinki 1952 marked the Olympic debut of the Soviet Union. Amid Cold War tensions, the Soviets set up a separate Olympic Village with their East European allies – pictured is the Bulgarian apartment building with portraits of Joseph Stalin and Bulgarian politicians Georgi Dimitrov (bottom left) and Vulko Chervenkov (bottom right). The USSR's first gold medal was won by Nina Romashkova-Ponomareva, who threw an Olympic record of 51.42m in the discus. The Soviet Union finished second in the overall medals table, trailing capitalist rivals the United States.

Getty Images

Soviet gymnasts

The USSR was a commanding force in the Gymnastics competitions at the Helsinki 1952 Games. Pictured en route to collect their medals are the Soviet women gymnasts, who, in the words of the official report, 'came out on top, overwhelmingly so' in the Team event. Mariya Gorokhovskaya was particularly successful, claiming two gold and five silver medals – setting a record for the most medals won by a female athlete at one Olympic Games. For decades to come, the Soviet Union would dominate the women's Team Gymnastics, winning at every Games between 1952 and 1988, except for Los Angeles 1984 – the only time the country did not compete, as it was the year of the Soviet boycott.

Time & Life Pictures/Getty Images

Emil Zátopek

Emil Zátopek's performance at the Helsinki 1952 Games is among the greatest in distance running history. The Czech superstar defended the 10,000m title he had won in London four years earlier, and won gold in the 5000m. The latter was a tight affair; Zátopek took the lead on the final curve (pictured) ahead of Frenchman Alain Mimoun (silver) and German Herbert Schade (bronze), after Briton Chris Chataway had fallen, exhausted. The same afternoon, Zátopek's wife, Dana, added to the family medal collection by taking gold in the Javelin. Incredibly, Zátopek also triumphed easily in his first-ever Marathon – resulting in a unique triple victory. The Czech was nicknamed 'the Locomotive' for his distinctive running style, characterised by rocking shoulders, a face crumpled with exhaustion and loud panting. When questioned about his ungainly technique, the Czech replied: 'This isn't gymnastics or ice skating, you know.'

Time & Life Pictures/Getty Images
CORR/AFP/Getty Images

Jean Boiteaux

French swimmer Jean Boiteaux – who had just won the 400m Freestyle at Helsinki 1952, to claim France's first Olympic Swimming gold – helps his father climb out of the pool; Père Boiteaux was so overjoyed by his son's success that he'd jumped into the water to embrace him. Congratulations were also in order in 1952 for triple jumper Adhemar da Silva (winner of Brazil's sole gold medal); long jumper Yvette Williams (winner of New Zealand's only gold); and Josy Barthel, who came first in the 1500m and gave Luxembourg its first gold in the history of the Olympic Games. Great Britain also managed only one first place, in the men's Team Jumping event in the Equestrian competition.

Popperfoto/Getty Images

Hammer Throw

An unidentified competitor hurls the hammer at Helsinki 1952, an event won by 20-year-old Hungarian Jószef Csermák, with a world record throw of 60.34m. The Hungarians have traditionally been strong in the Hammer Throw; Csermák took the world record from his team-mate Imre Németh, champion at London 1948 and bronze medallist in 1952. Hungary performed remarkably well at the Helsinki 1952 Games, especially in Football, Gymnastics, Swimming and Water Polo, and finished third in the overall medals table (behind the United States and the Soviet Union) with a total of 16 gold, ten silver and 16 bronze medals.

Time & Life Pictures/Getty Images

HELSINKI 1952

Jamaican medallists

Although Jamaica fielded only eight athletes at Helsinki 1952 (compared with 295 for the USSR, for example), the tiny Caribbean nation managed to walk away with an impressive five medals. Two of them came in the 400m: gold for George Rhoden (centre) and silver for Herbert McKenley (left) – no wonder they look so delighted. Also pictured is bronze medallist Ollie Matson of the United States. All three runners took part in the 4 x 400m Relay, an extremely fast race in which Jamaica narrowly defeated the US. McKenley claimed another second place in the 100m (an equally closely fought contest that required a photo finish to determine the result) and Arthur Wint added another silver to the Jamaican haul in the 800m.

Gamma-Keystone via Getty Images

Australian medallists

The medal winners in the women's 100m at Helsinki 1952: South African Daphne Robb-Hasenjäger (left, silver) and Australians Marjorie Jackson (centre, gold) and Shirley Strickland-de la Hunty (right, bronze). The Australian duo helped their nation become the supreme force in women's sprinting in the early 1950s. At Helsinki, Jackson took the 100m and 200m Olympic double in emphatic style, and Strickland-de la Hunty claimed gold in the 80m Hurdles while setting a new world record. The pair were tipped to win another gold each in the 4 x 100m Relay, but the Australian team finished fifth after a fumbled baton exchange. Four years later, on home ground in Melbourne, the Australian women did win the relay and Strickland-de la Hunty repeated her triumph in the 80m Hurdles.

Time & Life Pictures/Getty Images

Indian Hockey team

A Finnish girl in traditional costume congratulates the Indian Hockey team on winning gold in Helsinki. India defeated Great Britain 3-1 in the semi-finals, before going on to overwhelm the Netherlands 6-1 in the final. First played at the London 1908 Games, Hockey has been an Olympic fixture since Amsterdam 1928 – with India dominating for decades. The country won six consecutive titles between Amsterdam 1928 and Melbourne/Stockholm 1956, in which time the Indian team won 30 straight matches, scoring 197 goals and conceding only eight. India's last win to date came at the Moscow 1980 Games, since when Germany and the Netherlands have proved most successful.

Popperfoto/Getty Images

Robert Richards

Nicknamed the 'Vaulting Vicar' on account of his status as an ordained minister, American Bob Richards is the only man to have won two Olympic golds in the Pole Vault. Having taken bronze at the London 1948 Games, he was the favourite for the Helsinki 1952 Games and managed to overcome his team-mate Donald Laz on his third attempt at 4.55m – setting a new Olympic record by doing so. Richards repeated his triumph four years later at Melbourne, where he managed to better his own Olympic record by 1cm. He also competed in the men's Decathlon at the Melbourne 1956 Games, but injury forced him to retire before the finish.

Gamma-Keystone via Getty Images

Olympic neon sign

Signmakers prepare a neon version of the Olympic rings for the Melbourne and Stockholm 1956 Games. This was the only time in Olympic history that the Games were shared between two countries; following the Australian government's ruling that its quarantine laws could not be breached to allow in foreign horses, the Equestrian events were held in Stockholm. The year was a turbulent one politically: the 1956 Games were boycotted by Spain, Switzerland and the Netherlands following the Soviet invasion of Hungary the year before, and also by Egypt, Lebanon and Iraq as a result of the Franco-British intervention in Egypt during the Suez crisis. The People's Republic of China also declined to attend because of the presence of the rival Republic of China (Taiwan). On a more positive note, East and West Germany competed together for the first time as the United Team of Germany.

Time & Life Pictures/Getty Images

Alain Mimoun

The closing moments of the 1956 Marathon belonged, finally, to Algerian Frenchman Alain Mimoun. Then aged 35, Mimoun had competed in the two previous Olympic Games, winning three silver medals in the 5000m and 10,000m races, but each time coming second to the great Czechoslovakian long-distance runner Emil Zátopek (who was also the defending Marathon champion in 1956). In the end, Mimoun won the Marathon comfortably with over a minute and a half to spare; he waited at the finishing line for Zátopek, by now a great friend as well as rival, who, suffering from the effects of a recent hernia operation, finished in sixth place.

AFP/Getty Images

Water Polo battle

Despite subsequently being dubbed the 'Friendly Games', the Melbourne/Stockholm 1956 Games were not always harmonious. The Hungarian Revolution, raging in the streets of Budapest just weeks before the Opening Ceremony, was fresh in the minds of both competitors and spectators at the semi-final meeting of the Hungarian and Soviet Water Polo teams. The match was marked by violence on both sides, at one point Hungarian Ervin Zádor (pictured) being bloodied by an attack. The game, later known as the 'Blood in the Water' match, was stopped a minute before the final whistle, when the crowd, hurling verbal abuse at the USSR team, threatened to riot.

STAFF/AFP/Getty Images

Betty Cuthbert

Australian 'Golden Girl' Betty Cuthbert (third from left) was just 18 when she won the 100m sprint at Melbourne Cricket Ground in 11.5 seconds. She went on to win the 200m four days later, setting a new world record of 23.2 seconds, and secured a third gold as anchor in the 4 x 100m Relay. Cuthbert subsequently suffered injuries, but came back to win the 400m at the Tokyo 1964 Games – she's the only athlete to have won Olympic gold in all three sprint races. Cuthbert was present at the next Games held on Australian soil, Sydney 2000, when, wheelchair-bound as a result of multiple sclerosis, she was one of the Olympic Torchbearers at the Opening Ceremony.

Getty Images

László Papp

Hungarian boxer Papp was the first man to win three consecutive Olympic Boxing titles, taking the middleweight gold medal at London 1948, followed by the light middleweight gold at both Helsinki 1952 and Melbourne/Stockholm 1956. Undefeated in the ring, the southpaw was a national hero in Hungary, and as late as 1989 was awarded the accolade of 'best amateur and professional boxer of all time' by the president of the World Boxing Council. Papp's career came to an abrupt end when the Communist regime refused to allow him any further exit visas after 1964.

Getty Images

Vladimir Kuts

Multiple medal winners were de rigueur
in the track events at Melbourne/Stockholm
1956; home favourite Betty Cuthbert took
gold in the women's 100m, 200m and 4 x
100m Relay, a feat matched by American
Bobby Joe Morrow (often deemed the greatest
white sprinter of all time) in the same men's
events. The star of the Soviet Union was
Vladimir Kuts, seen here winning the
10,000m. It was the first gold medal for
a male athlete from the USSR, and five days
later Kuts again helped his country top the
1956 medals table with a convincing victory
in the 5000m race (ahead of Britons Gordon
Pirie and Derek Ibbotson). He won both races
in Olympic record times.

Getty Images

Chris Brasher

British runner Chris Brasher (third from left) chases Norwegian Ernst Larsen and Semen Rzhishchin of the Soviet Union in the 3000m Steeplechase. Brasher was first over the line, but was disqualified for having brushed Larsen as he passed him to take the lead. However, following an appeal (admirably supported by Larsen and all the other main runners), Brasher was awarded the gold – becoming the first Briton to win an Athletics gold since 1936. Larsen had to be content with bronze. Two years previously, Brasher had been part of the pacemaking team that helped Roger Bannister achieve the world's first sub-four minute mile; he went on to co-found the London Marathon.

Popperfoto/Getty Images

Closing Ceremony

Avery Brundage, fifth president of the IOC and a former competitor at Stockholm 1912, speaks at the Closing Ceremony in Melbourne. The event marked an important milestone in the history of the Games following the IOC's decision to adopt an idea put forward by John Ian Wing, a Chinese apprentice carpenter living in Australia. He wrote to the IOC suggesting that if the athletes paraded together at the Closing Ceremony, rather than in alphabetical order by country, it would be a fitting symbol of world unity. The tradition has been followed ever since.

Popperfoto/Getty Images

Wilma Rudolph

Wilma Rudolph's life would have been extraordinary even without her Olympic triumphs. Born one of 22 children to a family in Tennessee, she was lucky to survive childhood, suffering scarlet fever, double pneumonia and polio – which it was thought might stop her being able to walk. Instead, she took up running at the age of 12, and won her first Olympic medal (a bronze for the 4 x 100m Relay at Melbourne/Stockholm 1956) as a 16-year-old. At Rome 1960, Rudolph was unstoppable. The 'Black Gazelle', so called because of her elegant, long-legged running style, didn't just win three golds – in the 100m (pictured), 200m and 4 x 100m Relay – but won each of them in a world record time.

Time & Life Pictures/Getty Images

Cassius Clay

The career of American boxer Cassius Clay (right) is closely intertwined with the Olympic Games, even though he took part in the Games only once, in 1960, winning gold in the Light Heavy Weight class at the age of 18. Clay's shock win over Sonny Liston in 1964 (after which he adopted his new name, Muhammad Ali) made him the world Heavy Weight champion, but his legend was made by the gruelling comeback victories over Joe Frazier and George Foreman – both of whom were also Olympic champions – that followed Ali's ban from boxing for refusing to fight in the Vietnam War. Beset by Parkinson's disease in later life, a dignified Ali lit the Olympic flame to open the Atlanta 1996 Games, where he was given a replica gold medal to replace his own, thrown away in disgust when he returned from Rome 1960 to find he was still subject to racism in a segregated United States.

Popperfoto/Getty Images

Al Oerter

More than a brilliant athlete, American Discus thrower Alfred Oerter was an immense Olympic competitor. Not only did he take part in four consecutive Games (1956, 1960, 1964 and 1968) – a rare feat of athletic longevity itself – but he took gold, and set a new Olympic record, on each occasion. He managed to win in Rome despite having suffered a serious car accident in 1957, and again at the Tokyo 1964 Games despite such badly torn rib muscles that he needed heavy strapping. Oerter even returned from retirement to make career-best throws in his forties. Rome 1960 was good for winners across multiple Olympic Games: the Dane Paul Elvstrøm won his fourth individual gold in the one-person dinghy, Hungarian fencer Aladár Gerevich took his sixth consecutive Team gold in the Sabre (bringing his overall medal tally to ten), and Swedish canoeist Gert Fredriksson won his sixth gold.

Getty Images

Abebe Bikila

Ethiopian Abebe Bikila (one of Emperor Haile Selassie's personal bodyguards) won the Marathon at the Rome 1960 Games to become the first black African gold medallist, while running the entire race barefoot. He's pictured here a kilometre from the finish, ahead of his sole remaining challenger, Rhadi Ben Abdesselem of Morocco. It was a memorable event, ending beneath the Arch of Constantine in the dark, with the route lit by torches. By coincidence, this was also the last Games at which apartheid South Africa were allowed to compete; the country returned, post-apartheid, at Barcelona 1992. Bikila retained his title at Tokyo 1964 – just weeks after having his appendix removed – to become one of only two men to win back-to-back Olympic Marathons. His running career was cruelly curtailed by a car accident in 1969, but he returned to sport as a wheelchair archer and competed in the Stoke Mandeville Games.

Getty Images

Ralph Boston

A relative unknown before Rome 1960, 21-year-old Ralph Boston of the United States was on flying form during the Olympic qualifying trials of the Long Jump, beating Jesse Owens' world record of 25 years' standing with a leap of 8.21m – as pictured here. He went on to win the gold medal. Boston took part in the Long Jump at the two subsequent Games in Tokyo 1964 (where he won silver) and Mexico 1968 (taking bronze). He also managed to surpass his own world record a number of times, with a final jump of 8.35m in 1965.

Time & Life Pictures/Getty Images

Larisa Latynina

Winner of 18 medals (nine gold, five silver, four bronze), Soviet gymnast Larisa Latynina has more Olympic laurels to her name than any other competitor – male or female – in the history of the Games. This extraordinary achievement is all the more impressive given that she was competing across three consecutive Games (1956, 1960 and 1964), from the age of 21 to 29, winning six medals every time. In all the events Latynina participated in during the three Games, she only failed to win a medal of any colour in one – the Balance Beam at Melbourne 1956, where she finished fourth. Her compatriot Boris Shakhlin was also a phenomenal gymnast, amassing 13 medals (including seven golds) over the course of the same three Games.

Getty Images

Rafer Johnson and Chuan-Kwang Yang

American decathlete Rafer Johnson and his Taiwanese counterpart Chuan-Kwang Yang were college training buddies and close friends at UCLA, and contested one of the great Olympic Decathlons of all time at the Rome 1960 Games. Yang led his rival in six of the events, but Johnson was so far ahead of him in the discus, shot put and javelin that he had a few points in hand going into the deciding event, the 1500m. As expected, Yang finished ahead of Johnson – they are pictured at the end of the run – but Johnson managed to keep up with him during the gruelling race and thus won the Decathlon gold.
Getty Images

Arch of Constantine

The organisers of Rome 1960 were keen to make the most of the Italian capital's photogenic ancient monuments, especially as the Games were being televised live to 18 European countries and, a few hours later, to the United States, Canada and Japan. The remains of the Basilica of Maxentius, the Caracalla Baths and, above all, the Arch of Constantine provided backdrops to events, with the arch especially dramatically deployed for the evening finish of the Marathon.

Allsport/Hulton Archive/Getty Images

Fencing events

Italian épéeist Giuseppe Delfino scores a hit on Briton Allan Jay to beat him to the Individual gold medal at Rome 1960; the Italians also picked up the Team gold, with the British team taking silver. Putting Delfino somewhat in the shade was his compatriot Edoardo Mangiarotti, whose two medals brought his Olympic medal total to 13, six of them gold, between 1936 and 1960. Italy has always performed superbly in Fencing, as have Hungary and France. The 1960 Hungarian team also included a couple of impressive veterans, both Sabre specialists: 50-year-old Aladár Gerevich (first Games: Los Angeles 1932, Olympic medals: ten) and 48-year-old Pál Kovács (first Games: Berlin 1936, Olympic medals: seven).

Getty Images

United States Basketball

Basketball first featured at the Berlin 1936 Games, when the United States won gold. That victory signalled the predominance of the United States in the sport: the US men's team have won 13 out of a possible 17 Basketball gold medals to date, while the women's team have captured six out of nine (women's Basketball was introduced at the Montreal 1976 Games). The men's team that appeared at Rome – seen here playing the USSR, who won silver – have been described as the best amateur Basketball team of all time, containing as it did a host of future NBA stars, including Oscar Robertson, Jerry West, Jerry Lucas, Terry Dischinger and Walt Bellamy. Yet again, the United States won convincingly, without losing a game.

Sports Illustrated/Getty Images

ROME 1960

Yoyogi National Gymnasium

The Tokyo 1964 Games were the first to be staged in Asia. Keen to demonstrate Japan's post-war renaissance, the organisers commissioned some spectacular buildings – not least architect Kenzo Tange's Yoyogi National Gymnasium, with its swooping suspended roof, which hosted the Aquatics events. The smaller pavilion next door was used for the Basketball. Tokyo 1964 also saw the end of some old technology (the cinder running track, manual stopwatches) and the arrival of some new (fibreglass poles for the pole vault). In a gesture of reconciliation, the Olympic flame was lit by Yoshinori Sakaï, who was born in Hiroshima on 6 August 1945, the day the Americans dropped the atomic bomb on the city.

Getty Images

Dawn Fraser

Australian swimmer Dawn Fraser was the first Olympian to win three consecutive gold medals in a single event – in this case, the 100m Freestyle. Her first victory came in the Melbourne/Stockholm Games of 1956, a feat she repeated at Rome in 1960 (so becoming the first woman to successfully defend an Olympic title). She was then injured in a car accident that killed her mother, but managed to win an historic third gold at Tokyo 1964 – pictured here. The other swimming hero of 1964 was American Donald Schollander, who took four golds. It could have been five, had he been selected for the 4 x 100m Medley Relay, which the United States also won.

STF/AFP/Getty Images

Anton Geesink

In the two new sports introduced at the Tokyo 1964 Games, the host nation did extremely well. Japan won the women's Volleyball and took bronze in the men's Volleyball, as well as claiming three of the four available golds in the Judo. The fourth gold, however, went elsewhere. Dutch world champion Anton Geesink (pictured throwing Ted Boronovskis of Australia) defeated the three-times Japanese national champion Akio Kaminaga in the final of the open-weight category, thus denying the Japanese a clean sweep of medals – and the most prestigious of the golds – in the sport they had invented.

Popperfoto/Getty Images

Valeri Brumel

Although Valeri Brumel set the world record for the High Jump six times, he only took Olympic gold once, at Tokyo 1964. The Soviet athlete seemed to feel keenly the pressure of being the favourite, barely making it through the qualifying round, and the final was a protracted affair. His great rival, John Thomas of the United States, cleared 2.18m with him, but both athletes failed all three attempts at 2.20m. On countback, Brumel was deemed the winner. The USSR stayed just ahead of the United States in the overall medals table, but the US team won more golds. Little noticed beside this intense Cold War rivalry were Great Britain's Athletics victories, including the men's Long Jump (Lynn Davies), the women's Long Jump (Mary Bignal-Rand) and the women's 800m (Ann Packer).

Getty Images

Tamara Press

Soviet athlete Tamara Press reigned supreme in the Shot Put and Discus Throw at the Tokyo 1964 Games, taking gold and creating a new Olympic record in both events. At the previous Games in Rome, she had also been victorious in the Shot Put, but had come second in the Discus behind her compatriot Nina Romashkova-Ponomareva. Tamara's younger sister, Irina, was a versatile Athletics star too, claiming gold in the 80m Hurdles in the Rome 1960 Games and winning the Pentathlon – the first time it featured as an Olympic event for women – at Tokyo 1964.
Getty Images

Billy Mills

That the United States should reassert their
dominance of Athletics events at the Tokyo
1964 Games – bringing home 24 medals –
was no real surprise, but no one predicted the
winner of the 10,000m. By the last lap, only
three runners were still in contention: the
favourite (and world record holder) Australian
Ron Clarke, Tunisia's Mohamed Gammoudi
and an unknown American called Billy Mills.
Of Native American descent, Mills wasn't
even considered the States' best 10,000m
runner, but he surged past his opponents to
win in a time that shaved well over 40 seconds
off his personal best – and set a new Olympic
record. It was one of the great upsets in
Olympic history. Mills was only the second
Native American, after Jim Thorpe in 1912,
to take Olympic gold, and is still the only
American to have come first at this distance.

Time & Life Pictures/Getty Images

Opening Ceremony

From the jubilant Opening Ceremony on 12 October to the close on 27 October, the Mexico City 1968 Games were a huge success. But selecting Mexico City as the first – and still the only – Latin American host of the Olympic Games was a brave decision by the IOC. The city is at an altitude of 2,240m, so has 30 per cent less oxygen than is found at sea level – a cause for concern among athletes and coaches worried that the elevation would adversely affect performances, particularly in endurance events. It did, but it also aided sprinters and jumpers and meant that more world records were broken than at any previous Games. The Opening Ceremony also saw a woman light the Olympic flame for the first time, an honour performed by Mexican hurdler Norma Enriqueta Basilio de Sotelo.

Time & Life Pictures/Getty Images

Mexico 68 sign

The logo for the 1968 Games captured the spirit of a country, and appeared everywhere: on posters, stamps, signage, uniforms, balloons, street lighting, souvenirs – and as this large-scale sculpture overlooking the Olympic Stadium. But American designer Lance Wyman's logo wasn't the only memorable thing. New features included the introduction of gender tests for women; the use of synthetic material (tartan) on the Athletics track; and the arrival of the German Democratic Republic team, competing as East Germany. There were also political protests on the podium, and off: anti-government demonstrations by students ten days before the Games began, a reflection of political unrest around the world, resulted in a massacre in Mexico City's Plaza de las Tres Culturas that nearly caused the Games to be cancelled.

Time & Life Pictures/Getty Images

Bob Beamon

The high altitude of Mexico City benefited competitors in sports that required intense, short bursts of energy, such as sprinting, jumping, throwing and Weightlifting. The most spectacular achievement was that of long jumper Bob Beamon, whose world record-breaking jump of 8.90m (pictured) was beyond the reach of the official measuring device (an old-fashioned steel tape measure was used instead). The American's jump was more than 55cm longer than the previous world record, 60cm ahead of his nearest rival and set a world record that would last for 23 years. It even inspired a new word, 'Beamonesque', describing an athletic feat so superior to what has come before it is overwhelming.

Tony Duffy/Allsport/Getty Images

10,000m final

Athletes competing in endurance events, such as middle- and long-distance running and Cycling, were at a distinct disadvantage in Mexico City's thin air. The times for the 1500m, 5000m, 10,000m and Marathon were all much slower than usual, and African athletes used to running at altitude won all four events. Australian Ron Clarke was the favourite for the 10,000m, but found the altitude too much and collapsed on the finish line in such a terrible state that the doctor attending him was in tears; fortunately, Clarke recovered completely. Victory in the 10,000m went to Naftali Temu of Kenya, here trailing the silver medallist, Mamo Wolde from Ethiopia; Wolde claimed gold in the Marathon, while Temu was third in the 5000m.

Popperfoto/Getty Images

Deborah Meyer

Debbie Meyer, a 16-year-old high-school student from Sacramento, became the first swimmer to win three individual gold medals at one Games – for the 200m, 400m and 800m Freestyle races – no mean feat considering she had a severe stomach upset during the Games and suffered from asthma throughout her young life. She won each event by a large margin and outdid the achievements of her American team-mate Mark Spitz, who had come to Mexico saying he could win seven events (he won two, both relay races). Their combined efforts helped the United States take 21 of the 29 Swimming golds, but Meyer was unable to repeat this level of success and retired in 1970, aged just 18.

Time & Life Pictures/Getty Images

Black Power salute

In what remains one of the most iconic images of the Olympic Games, African-American sprinters Tommie Smith (centre) and John Carlos (right) protest against racial segregation in the United States. After accepting gold and bronze medals for the 200m at Mexico 1968 – in which Smith broke the 20-second barrier for the first time with a new world record of 19.8 seconds – the two removed their shoes, raised black-gloved fists and hung their heads during the playing of the American national anthem. Australian silver medallist Peter Norman wore a human rights badge in support of their protest. Smith and Carlos were booed as they left the podium, and were subsequently expelled from the Olympic Village. Both acted as pallbearers at Norman's funeral in 2006.

Time & Life Pictures/Getty Images

MEXICO CITY 1968

Vera Cáslavská

Czech gymnast Vera Cáslavská has plenty to smile about as she's thrown into the air by her team-mates at the Mexico City 1968 Games, where she won four gold and two silver medals, convincingly outdoing her already impressive haul of three golds and one silver from the Tokyo 1964 Games. She had also won a Team silver at Rome 1960. Victory in 1968 gave her more Olympic individual event titles than any other gymnast, and was a comprehensive trouncing of the USSR's gymnasts just two months after the Soviet invasion of her homeland. To the Mexican people, who identified with her stand against oppression, she became the star of the Games.
Getty Images

Dick Fosbury

American high jumper Richard 'Dick' Fosbury won only one Olympic gold medal in his career, but he did it at the Mexico City 1968 Games with a memorable and revolutionary technique that resulted in an Olympic record-breaking clearance of 2.24m. The methods used by previous high jumpers, such as the straddle, scissor jump or western roll, all involve approaching the bar from the front or side and taking off from the inside foot. The 21-year-old's curved run-up, taking off from the outside foot and leaping backwards head first, was initially rejected by the Mexico City judges, but they went on to accept Fosbury's innovative flop. It is now the discipline's most popular technique.

Getty Images

The tragedy of Munich

The darkest moment of Olympic Games history is captured in this image of a Black September guerilla in the Munich Olympic Village. On the morning of 5 September 1972, the Games were interrupted when eight Palestinian terrorists entered the Olympic Village, killed two members of the Israeli team and took nine more hostage, demanding freedom for several Arabs held in Israeli prisons. The Israel government refused, and later that day the hostages were taken to the nearby Fürstenfeldbruck military airbase, where a short gun battle ensued. All nine Israeli hostages were killed, along with five of the terrorists and one policeman. Less than two days later, the competition resumed after a memorial service was held in the main stadium.

Time & Life Pictures/Getty Images

Wilfried Dietrich

In one of wrestling's most famous photographs, West German Wilfried Dietrich throws his 400lb American opponent Chris Taylor during the Greco-Roman Super Heavyweight competition at Munich 1972. Taylor went on to take bronze in the Freestyle competition, but Dietrich failed to add another Olympic medal to the five he had already amassed – the most won by any wrestler. Dietrich had already competed in four consecutive Games (1956, 1960, 1964, 1968), winning medals in both the Greco-Roman and Freestyle disciplines; the high point came in Rome 1960 when he claimed gold in the Freestyle Heavyweight class.

Getty Images

Mark Spitz

Charismatic American swimmer Mark Spitz astounded the world at Munich 1972 by winning seven gold medals: in the 100m Freestyle, 100m Butterfly, 200m Freestyle, 200m Butterfly (pictured right – Spitz is fourth from bottom), 4 x 100m Freestyle Relay, 4 x 200m Freestyle Relay and by swimming the butterfly leg in the 4 x 100m Medley Relay. In eight days, he entered seven races, won seven races and set a world record in every one. What did he put his success down to? Well, he'd planned to shave off that famous moustache before the Games, but had done so well at the trials that he decided to keep it for good luck. Spitz's record for the most gold medals won at a single Olympic Games lasted for 36 years, until swimmer Michael Phelps, also from the United States, took eight golds at the Beijing 2008 Games.

Popperfoto/Getty Images

Time & Life Pictures/Getty Images

Mary Peters

In the 45th Pentathlon of her career, veteran British athlete Mary Peters achieved ultimate Athletics success at the Munich 1972 Games by winning Olympic gold with a new world record. The complex calculations used to work out the rankings meant that it was a nail-biting two days for the 33-year-old. She got off to a great start, with personal bests in the hurdles, shot put and high jump on day one to put her in first place, but a sleepless night and a below-par performance in the long jump on day two cut her lead. West German Heide Rosendahl, the local favourite, won the final event, the 200m, with Peters battling into second place, but it was enough for her to claim the gold medal. Rosendahl took the silver.

Popperfoto/Getty Images

Olga Korbut

Of the 7,134 athletes who took part in the Munich 1972 Games, the endearingly emotional Soviet gymnast Olga Korbut captured the public imagination with a spectacular routine on the Uneven Bars that turned her into a sensation overnight. As she put it: 'One day, I was a nobody, and the next day, I was a star.' The 17-year-old deserved it, not least for a daring approach to her craft that included moves never seen before, including a backward somersault on the Balance Beam and a backflip on the Uneven Bars that became known as the Korbut Flip. Mistakes meant that she failed to take the Individual All-Around gold, but she did win two individual golds (for the Floor competition and Balance beam), a Team gold and a silver (for the Uneven Bars) – and the hearts of millions. Back home in Belarus, she got so much fan mail the post office had to assign a special clerk to sort it.

Time & Life Pictures/Getty Images

Valery Borzov

Soviet sprinter Valery Borzov scored a double victory at the Munich 1972 Games, winning both the 100m (pictured) and the 200m – a feat matched in the same events for women by East German Renate Stecher. Two of Borzov's biggest rivals for the 100m, American sprinters Eddie Hart and Rey Robinson, were eliminated when they missed their quarter-final heats; US coach Stan Wright was using an outdated schedule, and thought the race was at 6pm when it was actually at 4pm. The Ukrainian won the final comfortably with a time of 10.14 seconds, a tenth of a second faster than second-placed Robert Taylor of the United States. Borzov also won silver in the 4 x 100m Relay. He was no longer so dominant at the Montreal 1976 Games, where he managed bronze in both the 100m and the 4 x 100m Relay.

AFP/Getty Images

Basketball final

The US Basketball team brought a 54-game winning streak to Munich 1972, and were obvious favourites to win gold. The team breezed through their first eight games to meet the Soviet Union in the final – the most controversial in the history of Olympic Basketball. With the match almost over and the United States ahead 50-49, a second was added to the clock after the Soviets claimed having called a timeout that went unheard. The USSR attempted a pass and failed, the time ran out and the Americans began to celebrate – as pictured. But William Jones, the Secretary-General of the International Basketball Federation (FIBA), intervened to add three seconds to the clock and the Soviet pass was taken again. This time they scored, to win the match 51-50. The Americans refused to accept their silver medals, and to this day have continued to reject the result and the medals.

Time & Life Pictures/Getty Images

Kip Keino

Kipchoge 'Kip' Keino (far left) vaults a hurdle on his way to victory in the 3000m Steeplechase at Munich 1972; fellow Kenyan Ben Jipcho came in second. Keino also won a silver in the 1500m, to add to the two medals he'd taken at the previous Games in Mexico City (gold in the 1500m, silver in the 5000m). Kenya, like Ethiopia and Morocco, has produced a long line of great middle- and long-distance runners and has enjoyed considerable success at the Olympic Games. This is especially true of the 3000m Steeplechase; since the nation's 1956 Olympic debut, it has won 19 medals (including nine golds) in the event, far more than any other country.

Time & Life Pictures/Getty Images

Alberto Juantorena

At 190cm and with a three-metre stride that gave him the nickname of El Caballo ('the Horse'), it's no surprise that Cuban star Alberto Juantorena began his sporting life playing basketball. But in 1971 he was persuaded to take up running and within a year was in the semi-finals of the 400m at the Munich 1972 Games, from which he was narrowly eliminated. Montreal four years later would prove a much more successful venue: Juantorena took gold in both a sprint – the 400m – and a middle-distance race – the 800m. He was the first, and remains the only, athlete to have accomplished this remarkable double. It was made all the more special by the fact that he had only seriously taken up the 800m that year, and his winning time of 1:43.5 was a new world record. And it was no fluke; he did it again in 1977 at the first World Cup of Athletics.

Getty Images

Daniel Bautista

In a Games troubled by financial problems and a boycott from 22 African countries (they were opposed to New Zealand's participation, because the New Zealand rugby team had toured in apartheid South Africa), there were successes for nations not well known for Olympic glory. Mexican athlete Daniel Bautista came first in the 20km Race Walk ahead of a strong East German field – his country's first gold, and the only one it won at the Montreal 1976 Games – while Heavy Weight boxer Clarence Hill took bronze for Bermuda. With a population of just 53,500, the tiny Caribbean island is the smallest nation ever to win an Olympic medal.

Popperfoto/Getty Images

Japanese Volleyball

Three new events for women (Basketball, Handball and Rowing) were introduced at Montreal 1976, but none produced as impressive a performance as the Volleyball tournament. The sport had been added to the Olympic roster for women at Tokyo 1964, when the Japanese had been victorious; they had also won silver medals in 1968 and 1972. The Japanese triumphed convincingly in Montreal, overcoming all their opponents easily, without dropping a single set. Takako Shirai – who had been part of the 1972 Japanese team – is the player being carried in celebration. This victory marked the end of Japan's superiority in the sport: apart from a women's bronze at the Los Angeles 1984 Games, the nation has not won a Volleyball medal since.

Popperfoto/Getty Images

Nadia Comaneci

At the Montreal 1976 Games, Nadia Comaneci became the first gymnast in Olympic history to be awarded the perfect score of 10 – and not just once, but seven times. So unprecedented was the feat that the official scoreboards weren't even equipped to display scores of 10.0; instead the Romanian's perfect marks were displayed as 1.00. The 14-year-old's incredible poise, imagination and skill made her the darling of the Games and brought her world acclaim, along with five medals, three of them gold. She added two golds and two silvers at the Moscow 1980 Games, giving her a career total of nine Olympic medals and the record as the youngest ever Olympic All-Around Gymnastics champion. She retired a year later.

Sports Illustrated/Getty Images

Lasse Virén

Finnish long-distance runner Lasse Virén carefully focused his training regime to peak precisely in time for each Olympic Games. The results were impressive. At Munich 1972 he claimed gold in both the 5000m and the 10,000m (despite falling during the latter race), then returned to repeat his achievement at Montreal 1976 Games; he's pictured in the centre winning the 5000m. In Montreal, he even came close to matching Emil Zátopek's 1952 triple, supplementing his two golds with a fifth place in the Marathon. Although Virén competed again at Moscow 1980, he was unable to add to his haul of medals.

Tony Duffy/Allsport/Getty Images

Vasily Alekseyev

To nobody's surprise, Soviet weightlifter Vasily Alekseyev won the gold medal in the Super Heavy Weight division at Montreal 1976, defending the title he had taken four years earlier in Munich – setting a new Olympic record on both occasions. Alekseyev was one of the greatest weightlifters in history, dominating his class for almost the entire 1970s and breaking the world record on numerous occasions. His failure at Moscow 1980 was a huge shock – he missed his first lift, which he had set too high, and retired from the competition.
Popperfoto/Getty Images

Misha the bear

Although the first Olympic mascot appeared at the 1968 Winter Games in Grenoble, Misha the bear, the mascot for the Moscow 1980 Games, was the first to attain worldwide recognition as a symbol of the event. As with most Olympic mascots, the bear was chosen for its strong ties to the heritage of the host nation and set a precedent for the ubiquity of mascots in the merchandising of sporting events. The band of Misha's belt is striped in the Olympic colours – blue, gold, black, green, red – and is fastened with a buckle in the shape of the Olympic rings. At the Closing Ceremony a representation of Misha shed a tear at the passing of the Games.

Getty Images

MOSCOW 1980

Opening Ceremony

The Opening Ceremony in Moscow's Lenin Stadium was a flamboyant affair, with performers creating elaborate human pyramids, but there was a distinct shortage of participating athletes. A boycott of the Games in protest at the Soviet invasion of Afghanistan in 1979, led by US President Jimmy Carter, meant that only 80 nations took part – the lowest turnout since 1956. Certain events suffered from the lack of competition, and it was no surprise that the USSR won most medals, followed by East Germany and Bulgaria. The boycott meant that all the original entrants to the inaugural women's Hockey tournament withdrew, apart from the USSR. Invitations were issued to replacement teams, including Zimbabwe, who selected a team less than a week before the Games and rushed to Moscow, where, to everyone's surprise, they took gold.

Getty Images

Sebastian Coe and Steve Ovett

Despite the boycott, Moscow 1980 still had its share of memorable occasions, including the battle between Great Britain's Sebastian Coe and Steve Ovett, the two dominant middle-distance runners of the time. Pictured below is Ovett (wearing vest 279) winning gold in the 800m, while Coe (254), the favourite, took silver, describing it as 'the worst race of my life'. The pair met again six days later in the final of the 1500m (pictured right), where Ovett was the favourite, but this time Coe delivered the upset, winning the race with a sprint at the last turn, with Ovett trailing in third. Coe retained his 1500m title at the Los Angeles 1984 Games – where the favourite was another Briton, Steve Cram – and is the only man to have won two 1500m Olympic golds. Since his retirement, he has worked in politics, as a Conservative MP and, more recently, as chair of the Organising Committee for the London 2012 Olympic Games.

Bob Thomas/Getty Images.

Miruts Yifter

The gold medal in the 5000m and the 10,000m at the Moscow Games went to Miruts Yifter of Ethiopia – seen here in vest 191 during the 5000m. Yifter had also taken part in Munich 1972, winning bronze in the 10,000m, but was unable to challenge for higher honours in Montreal 1976 because Ethiopia was part of the 22-nation African boycott that year (in opposition to the inclusion of New Zealand, whose rugby team had toured apartheid South Africa). Ethiopia has produced a slew of long-distance champions, including Abebe Bikila, Mamo Wolde and, more recently, Haile Gebrselassie and Kenenisa Bekele. The nation has been particularly dominant in the men's 10,000m, taking Olympic gold in 1980, 1996, 2000, 2004 and 2008.

Sports Illustrated/Getty Images

Allan Wells

Scotsman Allan Wells began his athletic career as a jumper, performing well in the Triple Jump and High Jump, but switched to sprinting after seeing Jamaican ace Don Quarrie in action. It was a good decision; at the 100m heats in Moscow he set a new UK record of 10.11 seconds, despite having to use starting blocks, which he disliked. Wells went on to win a very close final, sharing an electronic time of 10.25 seconds with Cuba's Silvio Leonard, but being awarded gold after intense debate over the photo-finish. He was the first British athlete to win the Olympic 100m since Harold Abrahams in Paris 1924, and was also, at the age of 28, the oldest winner of the title. Wells nearly scooped the double, but came a narrow second in the 200m behind Pietro Mennea of Italy.

Bob Thomas/Getty Images

Daley Thompson

Daley Thompson is one of the greatest decathletes of all time. His first Olympic gold came at the Moscow Games; the popular Briton had established himself as the top decathlete in the world and, with several of his main competitors absent because of the US boycott, he won easily. By the Los Angeles 1984 Games, Thompson had developed an intense rivalry with West German Jürgen Hingsen. Little separated them until powerful performances in the pole vault and javelin gave Thompson the lead. He had to run 4:34.98 in the final event, the 1500m, to break Hingsen's world record, but missed the time by 0.02 seconds – although he still took the gold. Two years later, the IAAF discovered that Thompson had completed the 110m hurdles one-hundredth of a second faster than recorded. One point was added to his tally, giving him a retroactive share of the world record.

Bob Thomas/Getty Images

Teófilo Stevenson

Historically, Cuba has been a powerful force in international boxing and Teófilo Stevenson – on the left, sizing up Soviet opponent Piotr Zaev in the Heavy Weight final at the Moscow 1980 Games – is regarded as its greatest pugilist. Notable for his height and elegant fighting style, Stevenson achieved the rare feat of winning gold medals at three consecutive Olympic Games (1972, 1976 and 1980), with just two of his Olympic bouts requiring the full three rounds. Following his amateur success, Stevenson was offered wealth, fame and a fight with Muhammad Ali to turn professional and compete in the United States, but declined out of loyalty to Cuba where sporting professionalism has been forbidden under the Castro regime since 1962.

STAFF/AFP/Getty Images

Opening Ceremony

After the financial troubles that beset the Montreal 1976 Games, only Los Angeles was prepared to bid for the 1984 Games. The first Games to have no public funding, the occasion was an impressive demonstration of American capitalist flamboyance, and set the pattern for all the Games that followed. Things didn't look promising at first: the USSR instituted a boycott as a reprisal for the US boycott of the Moscow 1980 Games, and most of the Soviet Union's East European counterparts also stayed away. However, a record 140 nations participated, and Los Angeles 1984 was carried by the exuberance and showmanship of its organisers – not least in arranging for Bill Suitor to fly into the Opening Ceremony using his jetpack. In the end, the Games turned a huge profit of $223 million.

Getty Images

Women's Athletics

After the women's 800m race at the Amsterdam 1928 Games, a debate ensued about whether middle- and long-distance events should feature in women's Athletics. Doctors warned that women would 'become old too soon', and female Olympians weren't allowed to run further than 200m until the Rome 1960 Games. Los Angeles 1984 saw the 400m Hurdles, 3000m, Heptathlon and Marathon contested by women for the first time (as well as Rhythmic Gymnastics, Synchronised Swimming and Road Cycling). Joan Benoit of the United States – pictured crossing the finish line in the Coliseum Stadium, where the 1932 Games had also been held – won the Marathon easily, leading for practically the whole race.

Bob Thomas/Getty Images

Mary Decker and Zola Budd

One of the most memorable moments of Los Angeles 1984 was the women's 3000m. Eagerly anticipated, it was seen as a showdown between home favourite and reigning world champion Mary Decker (vest 373), and a slight 18-year-old South African called Zola Budd (vest 151), famed for running barefoot. Budd was competing for Great Britain, because apartheid South Africa was banned from international competition. Halfway through the final, the pair collided when Budd overtook her childhood hero. Decker stumbled, fell heavily and, distraught, was unable to continue. Budd was booed by the American crowd, who blamed her (wrongly) for the accident and, shaken, finished seventh. Neither Budd nor Decker ever won an Olympic medal.

Bob Thomas/Getty Images

Carl Lewis

Until Carl Lewis appeared at the Los Angeles 1984 Games, no one had seemed likely to match Jesse Owens' magnificent performance at Berlin 1936. Just like Owens, the American won the 100m (pictured far right), 200m, 4 x 100m Relay and Long Jump. He never quite reached such heights of success again, but was still on top form at the next three Games. At Seoul 1988, Lewis came first in the 100m (due to Ben Johnson's disqualification) and Long Jump, and second in the 200m. At Barcelona 1992, he won gold in the Long Jump and 4 x 100m Relay; and at Atlanta 1996 secured a final gold in the Long Jump. Lewis's nine golds equalled Finnish athlete Paavo Nurmi's career tally, and in winning four consecutive Long Jump golds he matched Al Oerter's record for an individual Athletics event. Justifying his brash self-confidence, Lewis had become one of the greatest ever track and field competitors.

Tony Duffy/Allsport/Getty Images

Bob Thomas/Getty Images

Ed Moses

At Los Angeles 1984, all eyes were on one hurdler: the languid, elegant Edwin Moses. Moses had taken gold in the 400m Hurdles at Montreal 1976, in what was his first international competition, a month before his 21st birthday. He won that final by a distance of eight metres – still unmatched in Olympic history – and in a world record time. Few doubt that he would have repeated the feat in Moscow, had the United States not boycotted the 1980 Games: he won 122 races in a row from 1977 to 1987. Moses was victorious at Los Angeles 1984 (he also swore the Olympic oath at the Opening Ceremony), but it was his last Olympic gold, though he did manage to win a bronze – aged 33 – at Seoul 1988.

Sports Illustrated/Getty Images

Mary Lou Retton

With most nations from the Soviet bloc not competing at the 1984 Games, 16-year-old Mary Lou Retton of the United States became the first non-East European woman to win gold in an Olympic Gymnastics event. In a close contest with Ecaterina Szabó of Romania for the Individual All-Around event, Retton triumphed – by a mere 0.05 points – having scored perfect 10s for the Floor and Vault. She also claimed silver in the Vault and Team Competition, and bronze in the Uneven Bars and Floor, but Szabó took home four golds (for the Floor, Vault, Balance Beam and Team All-Around event). Romania came third in the overall medals table, with West Germany second and the US first.

Getty Images

Hodori
the tiger

The choice of Seoul as the host of the 1988 Games was controversial as South Korea did not have diplomatic relations with many Olympic countries at the time, and the event was boycotted by North Korea (supported by Cuba, Ethiopia and Nicaragua), after North Korea failed to gain co-host status. Despite this, the Seoul 1988 Games were a resounding success, devoid of the political difficulties of the past and with a record 159 nations in attendance. The official mascot was an affable tiger cub, who was given the name Hodori – 'Ho' coming from the Korean word for tiger (a popular creature in Korean legend) and 'Dori' being a common masculine diminutive.

Getty Images

Matt Biondi

There were two outstanding swimmers at the Seoul 1988 Games, one male, one female. Kristin Otto of East Germany bagged six gold medals – a record for a female athlete at one Games – in, uniquely, three different strokes (Freestyle, Backstroke and Butterfly). Matt Biondi of the United States tried to go one better, in an attempt to match Mark Spitz's haul of seven golds in 1972. He managed to win seven medals, but not all were gold: he came third in the 200m Freestyle and second in the 100m Butterfly. He was beaten in the latter race by just 0.01 seconds, prompting him to remark, 'One one-hundredth of a second – what if I had grown my fingernails?'

Getty Images

Florence Griffith-Joyner

Competing with fabulously painted, long fingernails and often in exotic, specially designed catsuits, 'Flo-Jo' was a media sensation – and also a superb sprinter. For the Seoul 1988 Games, the American was at her peak: she went home with gold medals from the 100m, 200m and 4 x 100m Relay, and also took silver (in the 4 x 400m Relay) to add to the 200m silver she'd gained four years earlier, at the Los Angeles Games. She also broke several world records. Married to triple jumper Al Joyner and sister-in-law of heptathlete Jackie Joyner-Kersee, Griffith-Joyner died tragically young, aged only 38.

Tony Duffy/Getty Images
Romeo Gacad/AFP/Getty Images

Greg Louganis

Widely considered the greatest diver of all
time, Greg Louganis took his first Olympic
medal at the Montreal 1976 Games, at the
age of just 16. At the Los Angeles 1984
Games, in front of his home crowd, the
Californian triumphed in the 3m Springboard
and 10m Platform – an Olympic double that
had not been accomplished for 56 years.
Four years later, in Seoul, he was up against
a younger crop of divers, but managed to
retain both titles, despite hitting his head on
the springboard during practice (the stitched
wound is visible here). Had he competed
at the Moscow 1980 Games – which were
boycotted by the United States – it's
possible that he would have achieved the
unprecedented feat of winning the Diving
double at three consecutive Olympic Games.

Pascal Rondeau/Allsport/Getty Images

SEOUL 1998

Olympic Eventing

Australian Scott Keach takes a tumble during the cross-country portion of the Eventing competition at the Seoul 1988 Games; the Individual competition was won by New Zealander Mark Todd, defending the gold he'd taken at the previous Games. Combining dressage and jumping with a demanding cross-country course, three-day Eventing is the most testing of the three Olympic horse riding disciplines. It was originally developed to prepare cavalry officers and horses for service and used to compare the military training standards of different nations. Equestrianism has a long Olympic history, debuting at the Paris 1900 Games, though women riders had to wait until the Helsinki 1952 Games to be allowed to compete.

Bob Martin/Allsport/Getty Images

SEOUL 1998

Olympic Handball

Handball was first played at the end of the 19th century in Germany and Scandinavia. It made its Olympic debut at the Berlin 1936 Games as an 11-a-side outdoor sport, but was then discontinued as an official discipline until the Munich 1972 Games, when it reappeared in its more popular and modern format, as an indoor game with a team of seven players. Women's Handball was introduced in 1976. Neither Spain nor Algeria (pictured) took medals at the 1988 Games; the Soviet Union won the men's competition, while the South Korean women's team was victorious on home ground.

Bob Thomas/Getty Images

Jackie Joyner-Kersee

American athlete Jackie Joyner-Kersee remains the greatest Olympic exponent of the Heptathlon, that gruelling two-day event that begins with the 100m hurdles, high jump, shot put and 200m, and finishes with the long jump, javelin and 800m. She claimed Heptathlon gold twice – at the Seoul 1988 Games (where she set a world record of 7,291 points, which still stands) and at the Barcelona 1992 Games – and silver once, at Los Angeles 1984. She also excelled at the Long Jump, winning one gold (1988) and two bronzes (1992, 1996). With a career total of six Olympic medals, Joyner-Kersee is equal fourth on the all-time list of Olympic medals in women's Athletics.

Ron Kuntz/AFP/Getty Images

Barcelona gold medal

The single flaming arrow shot by Paralympic archer Antonio Rebollo to light the Olympic Cauldron symbolised the mood of the Barcelona 1992 Games. It was politically the most tranquil Olympic Games for decades, even though the rump Yugoslav state was banned for its aggression towards the new countries of Croatia and Bosnia-Herzegovina (Yugoslavian athletes were allowed to compete as 'independent Olympic participants'). It was the first Games for 20 years to suffer no official boycott, and welcomed post-apartheid South Africa back to Olympic competition, as well as recently reunified North and South Yemen and East and West Germany. The break-up of the USSR meant its 15 constituent countries appeared under their own flags, but most of them competed, for the only time in Olympic history, as the Unified Team. As such, they topped the medals table, with Belarusian gymnast Vitaly Scherbo the outstanding performer, taking six gold medals.

Nathan Bilow/Allsport/Getty Images

Marie-José Pérec

Guadeloupe-born Marie-José Pérec – France's most successful athlete – is shown here winning the 400m at the Barcelona 1992 Games, the first of her three Olympic golds. Four years later, she became the first person, male or female, to win the 400m twice, defending her title in a time of 48.25 seconds, an Olympic record that still stands; she also came first in the 200m. An intensely private person, Pérec refused to compete at the Sydney 2000 Games, objecting to the intense media scrutiny that surrounded her much anticipated head-to-head with local favourite Cathy Freeman, whom Pérec had narrowly beaten in Atlanta.

Jean Loup Gautreau/AFP/Getty Images

Jenny Thompson

One of the greatest female Olympic swimmers, Jenny Thompson won her first medals – gold in the 4 x 100m Freestyle Relay and 4 x 100m Medley Relay, and silver in the 100m Freestyle – at Barcelona 1992. She competed at the next three Olympic Games, taking further medals at Atlanta 1996 (three golds), Sydney 2000 (three golds and a bronze) and Athens 2004 (two silvers). With a total of 12 medals, the American is third on the list of all-time female Olympic medallists, but she never managed to win an individual gold.

Simon Bruty/Allsport/Getty Images

Olympic Canoeing

Sprint races on flatwater in canoes (open-topped, steered from a kneeling position with a single-bladed paddle) and kayaks (enclosed, propelled from a sitting position with a two-bladed paddle) became a full Olympic discipline at the Berlin 1936 Games. The whitewater Canoe Slalom – as demonstrated here by German duo Manfred Berro and Michael Trummer – was added at the Munich 1972 Games, though it didn't return for 20 years until Barcelona 1992, when the United States took gold in the men's Canoe Double Slalom. This was an unusual result: there is a tradition of extraordinary European dominance in the discipline, with Europeans winning 90 per cent of the medals.

Bob Thomas/Getty Images

Derek Redmond

While British sports fans fondly remember the Barcelona 1992 Games for gold medals won by Linford Christie, Sally Gunnell, Chris Boardman and Great Britain's men's Rowing team, 400m specialist Derek Redmond has altogether more painful memories. The Briton had won gold at the European, Commonwealth and world championships, and came to Barcelona as favourite for the event. However, he snapped a hamstring halfway through the semi-final. Determined to complete the race, he hobbled around the track with assistance from his father, who had pushed past security to reach his son's side. The pair received a standing ovation as they crossed the finish line.

Gray Mortimore/Allsport/Getty Images

Nigerian medallists

Both of the Nigerian teams competing in the 4 x 100m Relay at the Barcelona 1992 Games took home medals: silver for the men and bronze for the women (from left to right: Beatrice Utondu, Faith Idehen, Christy Opara-Thompson and Mary Onyali). The next Games, Atlanta 1996, were the country's most successful to date, with two golds (for Football and Long Jump), one silver (for the women's 4 x 400m Relay) and three bronzes (in Boxing, and the women's 400m and 200m). Onyali took the 200m bronze, an extraordinary success for an athlete whose first race in spikes and from starting blocks was not until 1985, when she was in her late teens. Onyali participated in five consecutive Olympic Games from 1988 to 2004, the first Nigerian to do so.

Sports Illustrated/Getty Images

10,000m final

Perhaps the most dramatic single event of the Barcelona 1992 Games was the final of the women's 10,000m. Two-thirds of the way through the race, the white South African, Elana Meyer, broke away, leaving the whole field trailing (including the favourite, Briton Liz McColgan). But when Meyer glanced back, the black Ethiopian, Derartu Tulu, had calmly bridged the gap and joined her. For the last eight laps, Tulu remained on Meyer's shoulder, then forged ahead at the start of the final lap. Meyer could not respond and took silver to Tulu's gold. Since the Rome 1960 Games, South Africa had been banned from competing at the Olympic Games due to the racist apartheid policies of its government; in their moment of victory, Tulu and Meyer clasped hands and set off on a joint victory lap.

Getty Images

Brazilian Volleyball

The elation of the Brazilian men's Volleyball team, after defeating the Netherlands in straight sets to win the gold medal, is evident. This victory began an impressive streak in Olympic Volleyball for Brazil: either the men's or women's team has won a medal in every Games since Barcelona 1992, though the men had to wait until the Athens 2004 Games to reclaim their gold. The nation has done even better in Beach Volleyball (introduced at the Atlanta 1996 Games), winning more medals (nine) than any other country.

Karl Mathis/AFP/Getty Images

Opening Ceremony

The Olympic Games came to the United States for the fourth time in 1996, having already taken place in St Louis (1904) and twice in Los Angeles (1932, 1984). It wasn't a universally popular decision – many felt Athens should have been the host in the centenary year of the revival of the modern Games – and proceedings were upset halfway through, when a terrorist bomb exploded in a park next to the main Olympic site, killing one and wounding scores more. More positively, it was the first time that all National Olympic Committees (NOCs) – 197 in total – were represented, with many former Soviet republics appearing under their own flags. New sports included Beach Volleyball, Softball and Mountain Biking, and a women's Football tournament was also introduced.

Tim Clary/AFP/Getty Images

ATLANTA 1996

100m final

At Atlanta 1996, the 100m final was full of stars. Linford Christie of Great Britain was the defending gold medallist; Donovan Bailey of Canada was the reigning world champion; Frankie Fredericks of Namibia had run the fastest 100m that year; and Ato Boldon of Trinidad and Tobago had been the fastest in qualifying. It was a nervy contest, with three false starts (two by Christie, who was disqualifed). On the successful restart, Bailey was the slowest out of the blocks, but powered through the field to win in a world record time of 9.84 seconds; he was only the second person in history to hold 100m Olympic and world championship titles at the same time as the world record. Fredericks came second, Boldon third. The pair repeated their placings in the 200m, behind American Michael Johnson.

Simon Bruty/Allsport/Getty Images

Michael Johnson

Despite a stiff-backed running style that earned him the unflattering nickname 'the Duck', Michael Johnson ruled the 200m and 400m through most of the 1990s. His Olympic career peaked at the Atlanta 1996 Games, when he became the first man to win gold in both distances at a single Games – amazingly, Frenchwoman Marie-José Pérec achieved the same feat in the women's races on the same day. His stunning world record of 19.32 seconds in the 200m lasted for 12 years. Johnson might easily have claimed a third gold, in the 4 x 400m Relay, but injury kept him out of the winning US team (Johnson had taken gold in the 4 x 400m Relay at the Barcelona 1992 Games). The American's fourth Olympic gold came in the 400m at the Sydney 2000 Games.

Daniel Garcia/AFP/Getty Images

Svetlana Masterkova

At the Atlanta 1996 Games, Svetlana Masterkova of Russia became the first woman to win the 800m and 1500m double since Tatyana Kazankina of the USSR 20 years earlier. Having taken a three-year break from competition to overcome injury and give birth, Masterkova was not considered a potential medallist in either event. The 800m (pictured, with Masterkova leading) was expected to be a showdown between the great Mozambique athlete Maria Mutola and Ana Fidelia Quirot of Cuba, who herself had recently recovered from a near-fatal house fire. But the Russian led the field from the first lap; Quirot came second and Mutola third. Mutola finally won Olympic gold (Mozambique's first) in the 800m at the Sydney 2000 Games, in her fourth of six consecutive Olympic appearances.

Getty Images

Naim Süleymanoğlu

Naim Süleymanoğlu, dubbed 'the Pocket Hercules' for his diminutive stature (1.47m), hoists the bar at the Atlanta 1996 Games. Born in Bulgaria to Turkish parents, Süleymanoğlu defected to Turkey in 1986. Having taken gold convincingly in the featherweight division at the Seoul 1988 Games and Barcelona 1992 Games, he surpassed his own world record to claim victory in a closely contested event at Atlanta 1996 – making him the first weightlifter to win gold at three Olympic Games. He set an astonishing 46 world records during his career.

Popperfoto/Getty Images

Women's Hockey

Hockey is the world's oldest ball and stick game, with evidence of its existence in Persia as early as 2000 BC. The sport made its Olympic debut at the London 1908 Games and has featured at every Olympiad since 1928, but it was not until the Moscow 1980 Games that a women's event was introduced. At the Atlanta 1996 Games, South Korea (pictured playing the United States) came second behind Australia, who were unbeaten in the competition, with the Netherlands defeating Great Britain in a penalty shootout to claim bronze. Australia and the Netherlands have been the pre-eminent forces in Olympic women's Hockey, winners of three and two titles respectively.

Getty Images

Gail Devers

American sprinter and hurdler Gail Devers appeared at five Olympic Games – Seoul 1988, Barcelona 1992, Atlanta 1996, Sydney 2000 and Athens 2004 – despite having been diagnosed with an overactive thyroid (Graves' disease) shortly after her debut Games. She won three gold medals in all, for the 100m in 1992 and 1996 (both in a photo-finish) and the 4 x 100m Relay in 1996. She never managed to win a medal in the 100m Hurdles; agonisingly, at the Barcelona 1992 Games, she was well ahead but hit the final hurdle and fell, staggering to the finish line in fifth place. Devers' trademark was her brightly painted fingernails, worn so long that she had to place her hands flat on the track at the start, rather than braced on fingertips like all her rivals.

Mike Powell/Allsport/Getty Images

Cuban Baseball

After appearing intermittently as an exhibition sport from the early days of the Olympic Games, Baseball featured officially at five Games between 1992 and 2008. Cuba has dominated the event, winning three gold and two silver medals, while the United States, birthplace of the sport, has won gold only once. The Cuban team was victorious at Atlanta 1996 – pictured batting at the plate is star player Omar Linares – and didn't lose a single game en route to overcoming Japan in the final. In 2005, the IOC voted to remove Baseball from the London 2012 Games programme.

Rick Stewart/Allsport/Getty Images

Merlene Ottey

Merlene Ottey's Olympic career was exceptional – in several ways. She participated at an astounding seven Olympic Games between 1980 and 2004, more than any other Athletics competitor; and amassed more medals than any other female Athletics competitor, but never gold (three silver, six bronze). Her first medal came at the Moscow 1980 Games, her last two decades later at the Sydney 2000 Games, but she had most success at the Atlanta 1996 Games. There, she took silver in the 200m – pictured, with Ottey on the left and gold medallist Marie-José Pérec of France on the right – and also in the 100m (losing very narrowly to American Gail Devers), as well as bronze in the 4 x 100m Relay. Ottey represented Jamaica until the Athens 2004 Games, when she appeared for Slovenia, having taken Slovenian nationality a couple of years before. Astonishingly, at the age of 48, she was only a few hundredths of a second outside the qualifying time for the Beijing 2008 Games.

Getty Images

Alexei Nemov

Russian gymnast Alexei Nemov achieved the unusual feat of winning more medals than any other participant in two consecutive Games, at Atlanta 1996 and Sydney 2000; even more unusually, he won the same number: two golds, one silver and three bronzes. He also competed at the Athens 2004 Games, but by then was past his prime and didn't manage to place better than fifth. Two other male gymnasts have won more medals in total, both representing the powerhouse that was the Soviet Union: Boris Shakhlin (13 medals; Olympic appearances 1956-1964) and Nikolay Andrianov (15 medals, Olympic appearances 1972-1980).

Popperfoto/Getty Images

Opening Ceremony

'The best Games ever' was the verdict on the Sydney 2000 Games, where more than 10,000 athletes from 199 countries took part in 300 events – the largest Games at that point. Sports-mad Australia took the occasion to its heart, and Sydney was the perfect setting, with its beautiful bay, impeccable facilities and efficient organisation. The Opening Ceremony was a visual feast too, with Aboriginal dancers, fire jugglers, a 2,000-strong massed band, and scenes that encompassed the country's history, culture and landscape – including its distinctive flora represented by performers in illuminated costumes (pictured). Among the torch bearers (all female Australian Olympic champions) were Dawn Fraser, Betty Cuthbert and Shirley Strickland-de la Hunty, with Cathy Freeman given the honour of lighting the Olympic Flame.

Joel Saget/AFP/Getty Images

Leontien Zijlaard-van Moorsel

A champion cyclist in the early 1990s and a contender at the Barcelona 1992 Games, Dutchwoman Leontien Zijlaard-van Moorsel then dropped out of the sport due to problems with anorexia. She returned in storming form for the Sydney 2000 Games, where she won three golds – in the Pursuit, Time Trial and Road Race (pictured, with Zijlaard-van Moorsel on the far right) – and one silver, in the Points Race. It's the most successful Olympic performance by a woman cyclist. Four years later, at Athens 2004, she defended her title in the Time Trial and took a bronze in the Pursuit. The Netherlands has historically done well in the Cycling (which has always featured on the Olympic programme), but France, home of the Tour de France, easily tops the medals table.

Mike Powell/Allsport/Getty Images

Denise Lewis

Great Britain won an unprecedented 11 gold medals at Sydney 2000, its best result for 80 years. One came for Stephanie Cook in the first women's Modern Pentathlon, and two in the Athletics, for Jonathan Edwards in the Triple Jump and Denise Lewis in the Heptathlon. Lewis, who had taken bronze in the same event at the 1996 Games in Atlanta, was in third position at the end of the first day. After a strong long jump and javelin throw, she had been promoted to the top spot. She lined up for the final event, the 800m, with a heavily strapped ankle due to an Achilles tendon injury, but ran through the pain in a fast enough time to win the gold medal.

Mike Hewitt/Allsport/Getty Images

Haile Gebrselassie

Haile Gebrselassie is a legend of middle- and long-distance running, having posted victories and world records in almost every event. The Ethiopian had beaten his longtime rival, Paul Tergat of Kenya, in the 10,000m final at the Atlanta 1996 Games, and the duo were competing again at Sydney 2000. The two runners were shoulder to shoulder going into the final straight. Tergat (centre) pushed forward with a powerful sprint, but Gebrsellasie (left) managed to put on one final spurt and passed the Kenyan in the final metre – becoming only the third man (after Emil Zátopek of Czechoslovakia and Lasse Viren of Finland) to win consecutive Olympic 10,000m titles. Fellow Ethiopian Assefa Mezegebu (right) took bronze.

Darren England/Allsport/Getty Images

Ian Thorpe

In the run-up to the Sydney 2000 Games, the Australian media pinned its hopes on swimmer Ian Thorpe, aged 17 and 1.96m tall. On the first day of the competition, 'the Thorpedo' won the 400m Freestyle, breaking his own world record in the process. Just an hour later, he pipped Gary Hall Jr of the United States in a tense finish to the 4 x 100m Freestyle Relay. The American had taunted the Australians before the race, saying that the US would 'smash them like guitars'. However, in a shock result in the 200m Freestyle, Thorpe was beaten by Pieter van den Hoogenband of the Netherlands (Thorpe managed to overcome van den Hoogenband to take gold in the same event at the Athens 2004 Games). Thorpe is Australia's most highly decorated athlete, with a total of nine Olympic medals: five golds, three silvers and one bronze.

Joel Sagat/AFP/Getty Images

Maurice Greene

American sprinter Maurice Greene (centre) makes a flying start in an early heat in the 100m at the Sydney 2000 Games. It was an omen of things to come. The fastest man in the world at the time (with a world record of 9.79 seconds), he was the favourite for the 100m and won the final comfortably. The United States has dominated the men's 100m throughout Olympic history, winning 16 out of the 26 gold medals to date; next comes Great Britain, with just three winners. Greene also ran the anchor leg to take gold in the 4 x 100m Relay at Sydney 2000. Four years later, at Athens 2004, he could only manage bronze in the 100m, and the US also missed out in the 4 x 100m Relay, the team's clumsy baton passes meaning that Great Britain clinched gold by one-hundredth of a second.

Adam Pretty/Allsport/Getty Images

Dara Torres

American swimmer Dara Torres won 12 Olympic medals over the course of five Games, from Los Angeles 1984 to Beijing 2008, including two golds (in the 4x 100m Freestyle and Medley Relays) and three bronzes (in the 50m Freestyle, 100m Freestyle and 100m Butterfly) at the Sydney 2000 Games. She might have won even more medals, but she retired twice and so missed out on Altanta 1996 and Athens 2004. By the time of the Beijing 2008 Games, she was 41 – the oldest ever female Olympic swimmer – but age was no handicap: she claimed three silver medals, in the two Relay races and the 50m Freestyle, missing gold in the latter by one-hundredth of a second.

Al Bello/Allsport/Getty Images

Derartu Tulu

Derartu Tulu was the first Ethiopian woman to win an Olympic medal when she took gold in the 10,000m at the Barcelona 1992 Games.
She was nursing an injury at Atlanta 1996 and could only manage fourth; by the time of Sydney 2000, she faced stiff opposition from Britain's
Paula Radcliffe, as well as her team-mate Gete Wami (who had taken bronze in Atlanta). Radcliffe (left) shot off like a rocket and led for most
of the first 20 laps, but she couldn't maintain the pace and was overtaken by Tulu (right) and Wami (centre). At the bell, Tulu sprinted ahead
to beat Wami by five seconds with a new Olympic record; Radcliffe finished fourth.
Michael Steele/Allsport/Getty Images

Robert Korzeniowski

Robert Korzeniowski of Poland gives thanks after winning the 50km Race Walk at the Sydney 2000 Games, thus becoming the first man to win the Race Walk double; a week earlier, he had come first in the 20km Race Walk (after the original winner was disqualified). A supreme exponent of the sport, the Pole took three consecutive Olympic golds in the longer distance, in 1996, 2000 and 2004. Race Walking developed from 19th-century competitive long-distance walking, known as 'Pedestrianism', and first appeared as a standalone event at the London 1908 Games; the 50km distance – still a men's-only event – was introduced at the Los Angeles 1932 Games.

Bongarts/Getty Images

Cathy Freeman

A shell-shocked Cathy Freeman can't quite believe she has actually won the 400m at Sydney 2000. Freeman, an Aborigine, was the final Torchbearer and lighter of the Olympic Cauldron at the Opening Ceremony in Sydney. In the words of the official report, this represented 'what was to become an underlying theme of the 2000 Olympic Games – reconciliation between indigenous and white Australia'. Under enormous pressure from the Australian media and public, Freeman ran to glory in her distinctive full-body suit, designed to reduce air resistance, winning by four metres in 49.11 seconds. Her triumph was greeted with a standing ovation from the packed stadium.

Jeff Haynes/AFP/Getty Images

SYDNEY 2000

British rowers

The British Coxless Fours team – from left, Tim Foster, Matthew Pinsent, Steve Redgrave and James Cracknell – celebrate their win in the final at Sydney 2000. The British four resisted a late push from the second-place Italians to take gold, with Australia in third. It was a historic win for Redgrave, his fifth Olympic Rowing gold medal (IOC President Juan Antonio Samaranch rewarded him with a golden pin to commemorate the feat) and the culmination of a fantastic career. He competed at five consecutive Olympic Games, from Los Angeles 1984 to Sydney 2000, winning gold every time (plus one bronze) – a record for an athlete in any endurance sport. Pinsent, Redgrave's most frequent rowing partner, is close behind, with four Olympic golds.

Getty Images

Jonathan Edwards

Jonathan Edwards leaps to victory in the Triple Jump at Sydney 2000, a fiercely contested affair in which all three medal winners recorded their season's best distances. He was the first Briton to win the event since the London 1908 Games. Edwards had gone into the Atlanta 1996 Games as favourite and world record holder, but had to content himself with second place behind American Kenny Harrison, who set a new (and still current) Olympic record of 18.09m. But Edwards still holds the world record – a staggering 18.29m – which he achieved way back in 1995 at the World Championships; Harrison is the only other athlete to have jumped over 18m.

Mike Powell/Allsport/Getty Images

Opening Ceremony

Performers dressed as caryatids take part in the Opening Ceremony at the Athens 2004 Games. Traditionally, Greece leads the parade at the Opening Ceremony and the host nation follows at the rear; as Greece was the host in 2004, the country was represented in both positions, with weightlifter Pyrros Dimas at the front and the rest of the Greek athletes joining at the end. The Athens 2004 Games proved the most popular yet, with a record 201 nations taking part and a potential 3.9 billion television viewers worldwide. Construction delays had threatened to hamper the Games, but these were averted and Athens showed off a state-of-the-art transport system and some world-class sporting facilities.

Getty Images

Françoise Mbango

The West African nation of Cameroon has won five Olympic medals since it first participated at the Tokyo 1964 Games, three of which have been golds. Not surprisingly, given the country's success in the World Cup, one gold has been in the men's Football (at Sydney 2000), but the best Cameroonian athlete in Olympic history is Françoise Mbango, who took gold in the Triple Jump at both Athens 2004 and Beijing 2008. Mbango leaped 15.30m in the second round in Athens to take an emphatic lead. Tatyna Lebedeva of Russia, the favourite for the event, couldn't match her and finished third, though she did claim gold in the Long Jump.

Getty Images

Iraq Football team

The big sensation in the Football tournament at Athens 2004 was the Iraqi men's Football team. Despite continuing conflict at home, Iraq managed to qualify for the Games and then, on arrival, upset expectations by beating Portugal 4-2 in the group stage; here, Portugal's Cristiano Ronaldo (left) and Iraq's Haidar Abdul Razzaq challenge for the ball. They then defeated Australia in the quarter-finals, but lost to Paraguay in the semi-finals and finished a very respectable fourth overall. Favourites Argentina won every match without conceding a goal and took gold – a victory they repeated at the Beijing 2008 Games.

Getty Images

100m final

Yuliya Nesterenko powers to victory in the 100m final at the Athens 2004 Games. It was a surprise: the Belarusian had not been tipped to finish in a podium place, but she became the first woman to record times below 11 seconds in each round of the 100m. Silver went to Lauryn Williams of the United States, and bronze to Jamaica's Veronica Campbell-Brown. The Jamaican women performed exceptionally in the sprints at Athens 2004, with Campbell-Brown capturing gold in the 200m (as she did four years later, in Beijing) and as part of the 4 x 100m Relay team. Jamaica also took bronze in the women's 4 x 400m Relay.

Getty Images

Women's Wrestling

Among the sports introduced at the Athens 2004 Games was Freestyle Wrestling for women. In the Freestyle discipline (unlike Greco-Roman), competitors are allowed to use their legs as well as their arms, and can hold opponents above or below the waist. Here, Toccara Montgomery of the United States is flipped by Kyoko Hamaguchi of Japan in the 63-72kg division; Hamaguchi took bronze in the event. In fact, Japan won a medal in each of the four weight divisions. The nation impressed in general, coming sixth in the overall medals table: it performed particularly well in the Judo, Gymnastics and Synchronised Swimming, won bronze in the Baseball and Softball and picked up a couple of gold medals in the Athletics (not traditionally the country's strength), in the men's Hammer Throw and the women's Marathon.

Getty Images

Birgit Fischer

German kayaker Birgit Fischer's first Olympic appearance was on behalf of East Germany at the Moscow 1980 Games, where she won her first gold medal. It was the start of a phenomenal Olympic career: she missed out on the Los Angeles 1984 Games because of the Soviet Union boycott, but took part at every other Games up to and including the Athens 2004 Games. And won at least one gold medal every time. Fischer came out of retirement to perform at Athens 2004, where – aged 42 – she won gold in the K4 500m (pictured, with Fischer at the front) and silver in the K2 500m, bringing her total tally to eight golds and four silvers. Only one other woman athlete, Soviet gymnast Larisa Latynina, has amassed more Olympic medals.

Maxim Marmur/AFP/Getty Images

Shot Put arena

The return of the Games to Greece, the birthplace of both the ancient and modern Olympic Games, was an important theme at Athens 2004. Winners were presented with laurel wreath crowns (the traditional symbol of victory) and the Archery competition was held in the Pan-Athenean Stadium, which had been used for the Athens 1896 Games. The Pan-Athenean Stadium was also the finishing point for the Marathon, which was run along the same route as the 1896 Marathon. In another testament to the origins of the Games, the Archery and Shot Put contests took place at the Ancient Stadium in Olympia (the stadium's remains are visible in the foreground), the site of the ancient Olympic Games. Spectators were seated on the grass around the arena, just as they would have been in classical times.

Getty Images

Synchronised Diving

Lynda Folauhola and Loudy Tourky of Australia dive in the Synchronised 10m Platform at the Athens 2004 Games; they finished fourth. Synchronised Diving – where pairs of athletes perform identical or mirrored dives in the 3m Springboard and 10m Platform categories – first appeared at the Sydney 2000 Games. China, who came third in the overall medals table at Athens 2004, has dominated Olympic Diving in recent years. The country took six of the eight gold medals on offer at Athens 2004, although host nation Greece recorded a shock victory by winning the men's Synchronised 3m Springboard, the country's first Olympic medal in the sport.

Getty Images

Hicham El Guerrouj

Hicham El Guerrouj dominated middle-distance running for almost a decade, winning 83 out of the 86 races he contested in the 1500m and the mile. Unfortunately, two of the losses were Olympic ones, in the 1500m: at the Atlanta 1996 Games (where he fell just before the final lap and finished last) and the Sydney 2000 Games (where he took silver). The Moroccan finally tasted success at Athens 2004, managing to just hold off Kenya's Bernard Lagat. Four days later, he took gold in the 5000m, thereby becoming the first man since Paavo Nuurmi in 1924 to win the 1500m and 5000m double at the same Games.

Jeff Haynes/AFP/Getty Images

Kelly Holmes

Great Britain's Kelly Holmes gave up running to join the army at the age of 18, but watching the Barcelona 1992 Games on television inspired her to return to competitive Athletics. Much of her career was dogged by injury; she came fourth in the 800m at the Atlanta 1996 Games shortly after recovering from a stress fracture, and her training for the Sydney 2000 Games was also disrupted by injury, though she managed to take bronze in the 800m. Going into Athens 2004, Holmes was in perfect condition, and her fitness proved crucial as she triumphed in both the 800m (pictured) and the 1500m. At the age of 34, she was the oldest woman to win either event, let alone both.

Getty Images

Beijing National Stadium

The most talked about building at the Beijing 2008 Games was the National Stadium, nicknamed the 'Bird's Nest' – pictured with performers waiting to take part in a dress rehearsal of the Opening Ceremony. Designed by Swiss architects Herzog & de Meuron and Chinese artist Ai Weiwei, it was an engineering and architectural marvel. Equally innovative was the Aquatics Centre, aka the 'Water Cube', with its soap bubble-like cladding. But it wasn't only the modern side of China that featured: the Cycling Road Race followed the Great Wall and went past the Forbidden City, Beijing's 600-year-old imperial palace.

Teh Eng Koon/AFP/Getty Images

Athletics events

Kenyan Catherine Ndereba celebrates as she takes silver in the women's Marathon at Beijing 2008, as she had done at Athens 2004. The winner, by 22 seconds, was 38-year-old Constantina Dita of Romania, the oldest ever Olympic Marathon champion. No one country dominated the Athletics programme in Beijing; the United States, historically a commanding force, performed disappointingly (though still topped the overall medals table). The standout team in the track events was Jamaica, which won both the men's and women's 100m and 200m, as well as the men's 4 x 100m Relay and the women's 400m Hurdles.

APF/Getty Images

Michael Phelps

Michael Phelps was the youngest male swimmer – just 15 – to compete in an Olympic Games in 68 years when he swam in the 200m Butterfly at the Sydney 2000 Games (he came fifth). At Athens 2004, the American aimed to win eight gold medals; he failed, but came away with the still remarkable haul of six golds and two bronzes. Four years later, Phelps again entered eight races. He swam magnificently across all distances and disciplines, both Individual and Relay, winning gold in all eight events – the most won by any athlete at a single Games. He also broke an incredible seven world records. Phelps' place in Olympic history is assured: no one has taken more gold medals and only one other athlete has more medals overall (the indomitable Soviet gymnast Larisa Latynina, with 18 to Phelps' 16).

Timothy Clary/AFP/Getty Images
Getty Images

Elena Isinbaeva

Pole Vault superstar Elena Isinbaeva was unreachable at Beijing 2008. With a technique honed by years of gymnastic training as a child, she was the keen favourite: the Olympic champion from Athens 2004, the world record holder since July 2003 and the first woman to vault over 5m. The Russian's second jump was 4.85m, a height none of her competitors was able to clear. With victory confirmed, Isinbaeva had the bar raised to 4.95m and vaulted over on her third attempt. The bar was raised again, to 5.05m, which she again passed on her third try (pictured) – setting a new world record and smashing her own Olympic record by an astonishing 14cm. She has since vaulted 5.06m.

Getty Images

Michael Kappeler/AFP/Getty Images

Kenenisa Bekele

At Beijing 2008, Kenenisa Bekele defended the 10,000m title he had taken at Athens 2004 in commanding style, shooting ahead in the final lap (pictured) to win by almost 15 metres – and in a new Olympic record time. Fellow Ethiopian Sileshi Sihine came second, just as he had done four years earlier. Bekele proved he was on top form by easily winning the 5000m six days later. The two doubles (the 5000m and 10,000m at the same Games, and successive 10,000m victories) puts him among the all-time long-distance greats: only Lasse Viren of Finland and Emil Zátopek of Czechoslovakia have achieved the same. Tirunesh Dibaba also made history at Beijing 2008 by emulating her compatriot's 5000/10,000m win – the first woman to do so.

British cyclists

Great Britain dominated the Track Cycling events at the Beijing 2008 Games, winning seven out of a possible ten gold medals. A trio of these were claimed by Chris Hoy – pictured with Jason Kenny and Jamie Staff pedalling to victory in the Team Sprint event – making him the first British athlete to take three medals at a single Olympic Games for a century. Among the women's successes, Rebecca Romero won the Individual Pursuit, to add to the Rowing silver medal she took at Athens 2004 (she's one of very few Olympic competitors to win medals in different sports). In all, the British Cycling team captured 14 medals, a tally that pushed the country into fourth spot on the overall medals table.
Getty Images

Chinese Table Tennis

Chinese team-mates and training partners Yining Zhang (top) and Nan Wang contest the Table Tennis Singles final at Beijing 2008. Zhang took the match 4-1, giving her a fourth gold medal – she has won every Olympic event she has entered – but Wang is the most successful Olympic Table Tennis player to date, with four golds and one silver. Yue Guo claimed bronze to give China a clean sweep of the women's Singles. China's supremacy in Table Tennis since its introduction at the Seoul 1988 Games is overwhelming, especially in the women's competition, where it has won 11 out of a possible 12 gold medals.

Pedro Ugarte/AFP/Getty Images

Usain Bolt

Usain Bolt's extraordinary sprinting performance at the Beijing 2008 Games made him a worldwide phenomenon. In the 100m final (right), the Jamaican – known to fans as 'Lightning Bolt' – hurtled into the lead and was so far ahead that he slowed and began celebrating before crossing the finish line. Astoundingly, he still set a new world and Olympic record of 9.69 seconds. In the 200m final, the Jamaican ran flat out in his trademark gold shoes to break Michael Johnson's 12-year-old world record by two-hundredths of a second. Bolt made it a perfect Olympic Games with a third victory, and third world record, with the Jamaican 4 x 100m Relay team.

Pedro Ugarte/AFP/Getty Images
Nicolas Asfouri/AFP/Getty Images

Closing Ceremony

The Beijing 2008 Games were superlative in many ways. Despite concerns over China's human rights record and worries about pollution in the capital prior to the Games, nearly 11,000 athletes took part, representing 204 nations – the largest Olympic Games ever held. Many countries won medals for the first time, and some 40 world records and 130 Olympic records were broken. The United States took the most medals overall, but the host nation came second and won more gold medals. China spared no expense on facilities and organisation, and the spectacular Closing Ceremony was a fitting tribute to a supremely successful international event.

Getty Images

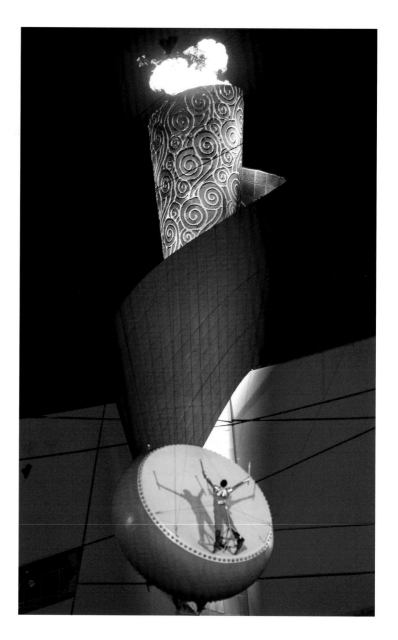

Competitors – teams

Non-competitors

Symbols